Five-Cent Miracle

ALAN GOLDSMITH PhD
with SUSAN FAUER

Cover photo by Susan Fauer

ISBN: 147822083X

ISBN 13: 9781478220831

Library of Congress Control Number: 2012912467
CreateSpace, North Charleston, SC

Dedication

As always, and above everything else, I'd like to thank the Almighty for my family, my life, my work, and allowing me to find the words to tell my story.

To my wife, Annie, whose inner and outer beauty have always enhanced my life.

And in Memoriam:

To my beloved parents (whom I miss every day), Louis and Esther Goldsmith, whose love, faith, and dedication to Dena and me formed the man I am.

And to my beloved grandparents, Hyman and Ida Paley, and Solomon and Sarah Goldsmith, who lived a Jewish life, and set the examples of humility, charity, faith, love, and laughter after which I patterned my life.

I also want to thank Susan Fauer for many hours of hard work and dedication to this project.

Foreword

By The Honorable Wilda Diaz, Mayor, City of Perth Amboy
(with Susan Fauer)

O nce in a lifetime, you may have the opportunity to meet an extraordinary human being. You read about these special people, see them on the news, and hear about their accomplishments. But to know one of these people close up is a whole different experience. To know someone personally who changes lives, moves mountains, and creates miracles is a miracle in itself. I know one of these people. He is a local guy, born, raised, and educated right in my hometown of Perth Amboy, New Jersey. Here is a man who has transcended city boundaries and brought his brand of heart to people throughout New Jersey and all over the world. He is Alan Goldsmith, PhD, President of The Jewish Renaissance Family of Organizations.

Even as a teacher and football coach at Perth Amboy High School, Alan was driven by his huge heart to mentor and guide the children under his care. During those years, he witnessed the transformation occurring in Perth Amboy. Townspeople started arriving from communities in Puerto Rico, Central and South America, Mexico, and the Dominican Republic. Times changed, American society changed, and our city changed. This evolving population needed help. And, Alan began to help. Now we see him, twenty years later, leading the Jewish Renaissance Family of Organizations, which provides a safety net of medical and dental care, vocational training, child care, GED guidance, and housing for our most underserved neighbors—and much more.

How can I describe Alan Goldsmith? I can simply say he is a loving, honest, and kind man. He embodies goodness and generosity. Alan leads with his heart. He thinks of others as an extension of himself, and he has dedicated his life to offering aid to many who would otherwise go without.

Alan Goldsmith is the "idea guy." He is the spark that sets things and people in motion. He knows how to assemble a powerful human workforce to push his ideas into reality. In the Jewish Renaissance Family of Organizations, he has built a huge cadre of talented, hardworking, and dedicated people. Even more important, Alan knows how to inspire and motivate them. He is the engine that gets the many parts and hundreds of people in the Jewish Renaissance Family of Organizations to perform miracles every day.

And then there's the laughter. There's no way I can speak of Alan and not speak of his sense of humor and ever-present laughter. Gales of laughter, hurricanes of laughter! Anyone who spends fifteen minutes with him ends up laughing, too. His sensibility for the lighter side hasn't diminished in the years I've known him. That's another spark he brings to his work, his friends, and our city. He promotes a serious agenda in a joyful manner. And Alan challenges all of us to keep up with him.

Alan is a man who perseveres. He has remained with his dreams in the face of financial obstacles, bureaucratic tangles, political quagmires, and personal problems. Eight years ago, when the medical center consisted of a handful of rooms in a tiny building on Hobart Street, no one could imagine longevity for this project. But Alan kept at it, made us all believe, rallied his many, many friends, and made it happen.

Two years ago, we witnessed the inauguration of the new medical center. The Robert Menendez Medical Arts Building sits just opposite the original small site in downtown Perth Amboy. This forty-eight-thousand-square-foot building also stands as a beacon, for it houses the Jewish Renaissance Medical Center, the first faith-based Federally Qualified Health Center in the United States. Serving Perth Amboy, all of Middlesex County, and the city of Newark, Alan's dream has become a reality—assisting thousands of people every month.

Alan Goldsmith is also a patient man. He is willing to do the hard work, dig for facts, and wait for information and results. Before he makes a decision, Alan will take the time he needs to listen to all sides. And I know that Alan is a religious man. So in these moments of introspection, I know he also relies on prayer and G-d to guide his hand and help him do this indispensable work.

It's been a long journey for Alan—growing up here, traveling far, and returning to Perth Amboy to teach, sell shoes, and then create the Jewish Renaissance Foundation. As our city changed, Alan found the way to change the status quo. Alan began reaching out to his neighbors as a teacher, and he's still reaching out and helping as president of what has grown to become the Jewish Renaissance Family of Organizations—helping on a scale no one could ever imagine.

The Jewish Renaissance Foundation, the Boys & Girls Club of Perth Amboy, and the Jewish Renaissance Medical Center (just three of the components of the Jewish Renaissance Family of Organizations) are the best things that have happened to Perth Amboy and its people. Because of Alan we have the resources and ability to take care of our townspeople; we keep families healthy. I always say, "Diseases don't discriminate." They don't care what language you speak, if you have insurance or not, or how much money you make. Now we can take care of our community correctly and comprehensively, thanks to Alan's heart, hard work, love for humanity, and guidance. I have known Alan Goldsmith for twenty years, and he still impresses me every day. To me he'll always be Mr. Perth Amboy.

* * *

Prologue

2004: West Orange, New Jersey

The sparkling skyline of New York City blinked its welcome to the tuxedoed, gowned, and bejeweled guests gathering in a banquet hall atop the First Watchung Mountain. This prime location in the Eagle Rock Reservation forest reserve occupied a site renowned for its unobstructed view of Manhattan's prominent profile. What a wonderful venue for this celebration. The glow of those distant skyscrapers added its decorative welcome to the partygoers. The twinkling backdrop of the eastern side of the Hudson River was glorious, yet as the guests gathered, it almost became inconsequential. Compared to the brilliance of the guests' smiling faces, the crystal and silver adorning the tables, and the cachet of the local and international dignitaries assembled at this sumptuous banquet, the Big Apple's glitter faded just a bit.

The guest of honor at this soiree was a New Jersey native…just a guy from Perth Amboy New Jersey, who, a mere eight years back, had pushed an idea into motion. His idea became a plan, and then a passion. As it took form, he named it to honor his heritage; the plan became known as the Jewish Renaissance Foundation. And this Foundation began offering comprehensive, compassionate, affordable medical care to the underserved population of his hometown. That idea has since grown; it has fed, housed, cured, aided, soothed, ministered to, and affected thousands of Perth Amboy's inhabitants, as well as people far, far from his hometown. This man began his personal quest of compassion in that city, and has carried it across the globe through the varied medical, social, family, and housing programs that have developed within the large organization it has become—the Jewish Renaissance Family of Organizations.

The Jewish Renaissance Family of Organizations' programs currently reach outward from Perth Amboy, throughout Middlesex and Essex counties, and beyond, crossing oceans to Ukraine, the Dominican Republic, Cuba, Israel, Hungary, the Russian Republic of Georgia, and most recently to the earthquake-ravaged island nation of Haiti. Pallets of medicines unloaded in the farthest reaches of the globe. Doctors trained foreign doctors on their own soil, and disbursed medical care and medicines under tents or in the nation's own hospital…to serve the medical needs of citizens of those countries. All that happened while the Jewish Renaissance Foundation was building a state-of-the-art medical and dental community health center to serve the most needful populations in Perth Amboy and Middlesex County; while opening medical centers in the Newark schools to embrace a generation of school children in need of basic health care; reaching out to their families and also offering myriad social programs in his hometown. This man's heart, compassion, energy, strong will to complete his tasks, charisma, charm, and ready smile were all being celebrated on this monumental evening.

Alan Goldsmith, President of the Jewish Renaissance Family of Organizations, was being feted for a new distinction on this evening in 2004. On this festive and brilliant night, the party guests celebrated another milestone, Dr. Goldsmith's induction as Goodwill Ambassador to the Intergovernmental Institution for the Use of Micro-Algae Spirulina Against Malnutrition (IIMSAM), a permanent observer mission to the United Nations Economic and Social Council dedicated to eradicating world hunger. How did this man come to this position in his life? Where did he begin? Where did he forge his ideas? As he traveled on his life's pathway, how did he come to be feted on this special evening? His story is unique and compelling. It is one of history, belief, commitment, and heart… above all, heart.

*At Highland Pavilion during the celebration of Dr. Goldsmith's induction as
Goodwill Ambassador to IIMSAM (United Nations). At Left: H.E.
Mr. Remigio Martin Maradona (Ambassador-Secretary-General IIMSAM);
Center: Ambassador H.E. Shariar G. Rahimi, Chief of Administrative &
Protocol Affairs, IIMSAM; and Dr. Goldsmith; 2004.*

* * *

Part I

"One People, One Heart"

The Heart of The Business

1

Russian Roots –
American To My Core

Being born in America is a gift for which I have always been mindful and thankful. I, Alan Goldsmith, native-born son of the stars and stripes, New Jerseyite from my first breath. Like anything and everything, my lot in life can be attributed to luck, circumstance, chance, kismet, the stars, or any other way that humans try to explain those things that occur to and around them. I don't think so. I have never felt that chance entered into my circumstances at all. Once I became conscious of my choices and of the infinite possibilities and outcomes of my actions, my life, and my path, I have attributed every step to *Hashem*, to G-d. He has guided my steps, including those first ones taken under the watchful eyes of my loving parents and grandparents. Since birth, I absorbed the smiles, hugs, words, songs, and customs of my parents and grandparents as they interacted with me, the new infant, that tiny baby…Alan Goldsmith. Surrounded by love from the moment I appeared in the lives of my loving parents, Esther Paley and Louis (Carl) Goldsmith, and filled with the language of my country, plus the syntax, song, and culture of my grandparents, Solomon and Sarah Goldsmith, and Hyman and Ida Paley, I grew into the man I am today. As I think about and recount my story, it becomes more and more clear to me that I have been placed on my *Derech Hashem*—my pathway through life—and guided by G-d to do what I do. There have been so many times, as I will explain, that it all could have ended or gone astray, but it didn't. I didn't. I am here, now, telling my story from these very small beginnings up to the present day. From a tiny American baby, born of Russian roots, to the head of The Jewish Renaissance Family of Organizations, this is my road, with guideposts, from G-d.

* * *

2

The Goldsmiths Of Vilna

*I*t was during the time of the massive emigrations from Eastern and Western Europe, around the beginning of the twentieth century that my own grandparents decided to leave all that they had ever known to journey far from their homes. We know so many of the stories told to us personally and publicized in the media of the tremendous forces that pushed simple people from small villages to travel such long distances. The reasons for such upheaval are as many as there are people who made that arduous and long journey. Although many ended up in other European countries, North Africa, South America, or Cuba, my forebears made America their final stop.

As told to me, Solomon and Sarah, along with their families, ran for their lives from the onslaught of hatred and religious intolerance that befell so many of their Jewish countrymen in the Vilnius region of (what was at that time) Russia. The Czar had no mercy, nor did his troops. The Cossacks, the Czar's henchmen, are so well known today for those acts of senseless violence that we have seen depicted in movies and popular fiction. With no inclination to dispense mercy and no checks on their actions, they terrorized Jewish peasants, my grandparents among them. So Solomon and Sarah fled their homeland, terrified of the Cossacks and their ruthless and merciless actions during the Czar's pogroms. Solomon and Sarah ran in search of safety and a new life.

They escaped all the way to Sweden. Simple people that they were, they had no idea how far the influence of the Czar extended. They were still terrified that somehow the mighty Czar and his Cossack troops could track them. It was for this reason they took a surname off a tombstone in a Jewish Swedish cemetery. And so, the Goldsmith family came to be named. Solomon's brother took another name from the stones and became a Neimark. Eventually, the Russian Goldsmiths and Neimarks continued on to Malmö, Sweden, where my father, Louis, was born. I always found it interesting that his name changed. He was named Carl in Sweden, land of his birth, and later became Louis. Six months after his birth, Grandpa Solomon, Grandmother Sarah, and Solomon's sister Rose crossed the Atlantic to America, carrying Carl. Solomon's brother, the patriarch of the Neimark clan of Sweden, didn't make that trip. He remained in Malmö, where that branch of our family still resides.

* * *

3

The Goldsmiths Arrive—
Perth Amboy

After the long journey, my family established itself in Perth Amboy. My grandparents settled here, put down roots, and began their American lives. They couldn't bring many belongings with them, but my Grandfather Solomon brought his trade. Once a Russian shoemaker, now he was an American shoemaker. Around 1916 my grandpop started fixing shoes in a barn on Fayette Street. In those early days of the last century, horses still pulled produce and goods around town through the cobblestone avenues. I have always tried to picture him, so young with so many expectations for his new life, hammering away amid straw and horses. When he began repairing shoes in America, I was told he had a few pairs of shoes in the back for sale, too.

Solomon eventually shifted his focus from repairing worn-out shoes to selling new shoes. He established the Goldsmith Shoe Store, a business that grew and allowed the Goldsmith family to prosper. There was a place for my dad there. He worked with his father before being drafted into service during World War II. He left to fight in the early years of the war, and returned in 1946 to rejoin his father in the family business. He took off his uniform and put on the mantle of the shoe salesman. By that time, the store had moved around the corner from Fayette Street to its new home. Together, my grandfather and father labored in the Goldsmith Shoe Store on State Street. The business was a going concern; working side by side, my father and grandfather built it into a successful business.

* * *

4
Goldsmith Shoe Store

I love thinking about what the store may have been like in those early years. My images stem from the stories recited to me by my father and grandfather. So I know that when Grandpop Solomon Goldsmith began selling shoes on State Street, he still plied his original trade, fixing and repairing. After all, he was still a shoemaker. Eventually, Grandpop even hired a friend of his who was a podiatry student to work from the back of the store. Things were certainly different then.

My earliest memories of the store remain vivid. Grandpop had racks and shelves of shoes set up on the right and left sides of the front door. He did keep some in the back room, but customers could see most of the stock right there. Up near the front of the store was a desk and big metal cash register. I even remember that there was a Mother Goose lamp in the back. Maybe that was the children's section, or something to indicate that children's shoes were sold there.

Grandpop Goldsmith passed away in 1955. He had lived with diabetes. He had no health insurance. Who knows what kind of care he had been receiving. On his way home from *shul* (synagogue), he suffered a heart attack. He fell and was taken to the hospital, where he died.

Things began changing on State Street when a developer arrived and began buying up all the stores. Change brought an apartment building to that block; it's still there today where the original store stood. My father took the money from that sale and bought a store at a different location on the same thoroughfare, closer to Smith Street. Goldsmith Shoes reopened at 323 State Street.

Dr. Goldsmith's parents at the Grand Opening of Goldsmith Shoe Store, 323 State St, Perth Amboy, 1961.

Alan's sister Dena, Grandpa Hymie, and Alan at shoe store Grand Opening, 1961.

The Goldsmith Shoe Store had a brand new look, with two gigantic windows looking out onto State Street. A big vestibule opened up right inside the front door and extended about twenty feet in, which led to the main part of the store. Men's shoes were displayed and stored on one side of this room and women's on the other. The cash register was located on the left side, near the men's shoes. Like so many shoe stores of that era, the back-to-back chairs marched in a row from the front to the rear (down the middle) of the main room.

Dad's store did have a small area for adjustments, but not repairs. He could stretch a shoe, put in metatarsals or heel pads, simple things like that. In those "olden days," dad's store had a cantankerous boiler that often broke. Since there were only two old radiators near the front door, it was always a bit chilly in the store anyway, even when the boiler was cranking away. Mom and dad suffered through their own personal indoor winters. Eventually the gas company put in a line so Goldsmith Shoes could have a hot air system. It warmed up then.

I eventually worked with my dad in that store, and he taught me everything I needed to know to sell shoes. The hardest thing for me was learning how to properly measure the foot. My dad was an expert at that. He could just look at a person's foot and know his size. He had been at this for so long. He taught me the importance of measuring; he insisted that we go farther to assure our customers of a properly fitted shoe.

When I was just beginning with him in the early 80s, I actually did fit a customer incorrectly one day. My dad compensated for my mistake, took the shoes back, and made sure that the customer received a correctly fitting shoe. Dad was a stickler for doing it correctly. I got it too, finally. Again, the lessons from my father, even when I was an adult, simply underscored the messages I had originally received as a child…fairness, treating people kindly, extending yourself, and dealing from the heart. When I ran the store, I just continued doing what I was taught. Not only was it right, but it brought customers back again and again.

* * *

5

The Paleys Of Minsk Reach Perth Amboy

y mother's parents, Hyman and Ida, fled Minsk during the horrible time of murder and persecution by the Cossacks that erupted at the end of the nineteenth century. I think Hyman and Ida came from the same general area, but did not know one another in Russia. They came from what was called the Pale, a large area that included the territory of what is now Eastern Europe. In the late 1700s, Czar Catherine The Great had forced the Jews to relocate and live there. Thus came my grandfather's surname, Dov Hymie from the Pale. They, like the Goldsmiths, made the long journey to America. Hyman and Ida met and married in their new land, and my mother, Esther, was born in 1920 in Woodbridge, New Jersey. So many Americans can recite a story similar to mine. Whether the route began in Ireland, or Italy or Poland or Rumania,

America was the destination. I can trace my lineage through that tidal wave of humanity back to the *shtetls* (small towns) of Russia.

Hyman and Ida arrived with the hordes of Europeans who filtered into the cities of America after disembarking in New York Harbor. Some who stayed on the East Coast settled in Manhattan's Lower East Side, some ventured into Brooklyn neighborhoods, and others moved into New Jersey.

The Paleys ultimately settled in Perth Amboy. Hyman made a home with his young wife on Hall Avenue, an area inhabited by so many other immigrants. It almost seems like my grandparents and those who came from so far away tried to recreate the village atmosphere they knew. The area around Hall Avenue was predominantly Polish. That meant that Ida's first language learned here in America was not English, but Polish. She was fluent in various languages, Lithuanian and Russian among them, to which she added Polish in her new home. Of course, Ida eventually added English to the garden of languages she cultivated.

My Grandpa Hymie, a barber in Russia, became a barber in America. From Hall Avenue, the Paleys moved to Gordon Avenue, which was around the corner from the Goldsmith home. In those beginning years for the American Paleys, Perth Amboy continued to be a destination for many immigrants who crossed the Atlantic Ocean and then the Hudson River, searching for a home. Those waves of new inhabitants made Perth Amboy a vibrant growing city at the beginning of the twentieth century. Many Eastern European languages echoed around town in those years.

My story continues with the marriage of my parents, Louis Goldsmith and Esther Paley, who married before the outbreak of World War II. I was born in 1947, and was named for my Great-grandfather Paley, Ahvraham Yosuf.

* * *

6

Setting The Example

O ne after another, there were examples and moments when my grandparents demonstrated concern for their fellow men. My Grandfather Solomon, for instance, even lived this truth through his business. If someone came into his shoe store who needed shoes and couldn't afford to buy them, he found a way to help...always. Last year's models became gifts to needy children with no shoes.

Grandpa Hymie often opened his home to any and everyone needing a meal, a place to rest, a friend. People were always coming in and out of his house. Anyone in need only had to let Hymie know. I remember that he had a vegetable garden out back and was always giving fresh food to hungry people. I always imagined that my grandparents learned the act of kindness themselves in Russia and merely brought this love and concern with them.

I look like my Grandpa Hymie. If you put his picture as a young man side by side with mine at eighteen or nineteen, you'd swear we were identical twins. At a quick glance, he was me, with a little moustache.

Hymie Paley was my beloved grandpa, known to me as Peepop, the barber, the believer in *Tzedakah* (charity), the joker, the buoyant, happy soul. He brought his tonsorial skills with him in his escape from religious repression from the Cossacks to a new world of freedom. Not only did he bring his talent (his livelihood), but he brought with him from Russia his heart, his good soul.

He and Ida were deeply involved in the Jewish community in Perth Amboy. They were tightly connected to their orthodox synagogue; in fact, they helped start the Hillel Academy. They made sure I went to Yiddish school; it was called *Shalom Aleichem*. They were also instrumental in aiding the startup of the synagogue. Growing up around them, I learned a great deal about being Jewish. I learned about my heritage.

Grandpa Hymie was always collecting money for Israel on behalf of the Jewish National Fund. My first lessons in giving started here. There was always a *pushke*, a collection box, in his house. On *shabbos* (Friday nights) he encouraged his grandchildren to put in a penny, a nickel, or whatever we could. He was always giving, always thinking of others, always setting the example. And he offered this generosity from his loving soul and never wanted anything in return. From Grandpa Hymie, I learned the trick to giving from the heart: "Put the money under the door and run away."

* * *

7

Grandpa Hymie
And The Nickel

*T*he quiet streets of residential Perth Amboy still look the about the same as they did when I was a little boy. Slightly removed from the bustle of downtown, the single-family and two-family homes each occupied a tiny piece of fenced property giving the neighborhood a neat look. Life hummed along in a predictable quiet tempo around my elementary, Number 7 School. On one particular Friday afternoon in 1954, the usual quiet burst wide apart with the end of the school day.

The dismissal bell's echo rocked the cavernous halls of the school. Freedom! Even as a second grader, I knew that bell gave us permission to cut loose. I ran out of my classroom into the hallway mob, and down the brick steps into the balmy afternoon sunshine. Hundreds of feet pounded with mine. Joyous screams pierced the tranquil streets as we galloped to our weekend liberty. There was still plenty of sunshine left for us to play and fool around and, for me in particular, to spend time with my Peepop. I knew I would meet my Grandpa Hymie there on the sidewalk. What I didn't know, as I ran into his loving arms, was that this one very special Friday afternoon would become a marker and a guidepost for me, and would serve to lead me for the rest of my life. I ran to grab and hug my Grandpa Hymie Paley, my Friday afternoon companion...my Friday guy. He laughed and fussed when I charged him and threw myself into his arms.

He and I spent special time together most Friday afternoons when my mom and dad worked into the approaching Sabbath. The necessities of running their shoe store gave my sister Dena and me wonderful, long, lazy Fridays to spend with my grandparents at their home. And this Friday, this very special Sabbath eve, Peepop and I met once again outside my school.

Grandpa Hymie bent down and wrapped me in his strong arms. He squeezed me deep into his embrace, kissed my chubby smiling cheek, and said, "Hello, boychik." He was my Peepop and I was his "boychik," endearing terms that defined the huge love and respect and happiness we both felt. Peepop took my little hand in his big square one, and with an extra squeeze, we set off walking. The sun, still well above the horizon, cast our shadows long on the warm sidewalk. Our voices punctuated the breezy afternoon, and the swishing leaves of the huge oaks lining the quiet streets played their hushed tune like a loving serenade to our conversation. We strolled slowly through our neighborhood. Traffic, as always, was light. So our quiet words were never interrupted, even as the random Dodge or sleek Chrysler sedan purred past us. Our feet slapped a regular cadence into the afternoon sounds of residential Perth Amboy that Friday, as they had on so many other Sabbath afternoons. His big shoes drummed out a slow beat, and my little shoes tippety-tapped the counter-rhythm. Bippity-bippity, bop, bop. Bippity-bippity, bop, bop. He walked slowly with his grandpa-beat as I skittered my own cadence into our syncopation on the cement sidewalk. And so we strolled.

I knew that the Sabbath was approaching. And I knew that Peepop and I had some time left to ourselves in the dwindling light of the day, before we began the ritual meal and chanting the prayers to welcome sundown.

My little heart skipped along with my noisy feet on this particular Friday, because today Peepop said we were going to the candy store. Grandpa Hymie whispered to me that we were making a little detour to buy me some sweets. Now I had an extra reason to celebrate this warm and happy Sabbath! Our clicking heels were now headed in the direction of the candy store on the corner of Paterson and Madison. This was *the* place for the kids from my school to purchase their Turkish Taffy, Mary Janes, and Clark Bars, long paper sheets of sugar dots, and tiny wax bottles filled with sugar-syrup. Now it was my turn. I probably tugged a bit at Peepop's patient hand, as we walked the leafy shaded streets in that direction.

Grandpa Hymie dug into the pocket of his jacket, and that memory is still vivid. His head was slightly tilted, and the worn hat that always perched on his graying head partially hid his sweet face from me. But even without seeing it, I knew he was smiling. He was always smiling at and with me. He drew his hand from the folds of his jacket and placed a big shiny nickel into my free hand. My smile grew even bigger. And I jumped a little dance of satisfaction, then fell back into our stroll. A nickel for candy was a big deal. Not only was it a special moment, but I could buy a surprising amount of treats with that coin. In my little-boy mind, I now had a special power in the form of that shiny piece of metal clutched into my little fist.

Our voices continued to rise and fall in the lively conversation between us. Peepop's heavily accented English substituted the V's and W's, and rounded out the vowels, while my squeaky youthful voice lilted with the sounds of New Jersey woven through. Two generations, two melodies, one song. We walked into the sinking sun, into the glowing afternoon, into the muted sounds of a town winding down into the Sabbath. And we were headed to the candy store to buy me some candy. A golden moment for a seven-year-old.

As we turned the corner on the shady street near the candy store, we saw a man in front of a building. He sat in a wheelchair parked near the wall. As we approached, we could see he had no legs; he was trapped in that chair. He sat quietly in the shade with a cup of pencils in one hand.

Grandpa Hymie slowed down, and I held back with him. He bent down so his face was even with mine. He put his whiskered face so close, his eyes glowed big in front of me. Then he placed his soft lips to my ear. His whisper tickled a bit as he said, "Boychik, do you see that man over there?" Of course I did, and I whispered this to him, tickling myself on the wisps of hair curling out from under his hat. "What are you going to do with that nickel I gave you?" he asked me. I was ready for that one. I knew just what I was going to do with my nickel. "Grandpa, I'm gonna get some candy," I whispered excitedly. I loved fudge, and I could already taste my treat. He bent even lower and whispered even more quietly so it sounded like a dream. "I know you like candy, but see that man, boychik? He needs help. What do you think you should do?" Such a question from the man I loved with all my heart! All I could hear was the booming silence as he waited. I knew what he would do, and I knew what he wanted me to do. I didn't feel terribly convinced about this turn of events, but I loosened my hand from Grandpa's, turned away, and walked up to the man. My Buster Browns made determined clicking sounds on that quiet street. I stopped in front of this old man, and I dropped my nickel fortune into his metal cup. My fudge dreams disappeared as the coin clinked to the bottom. I loved, loved, loved fudge...but I loved my Peepop more. His praise meant even more to me than yummy chocolate. So I parted with my nickel.

I remember the astonished look on the face of that disabled man. He stared at me in amazement, and turned his gaze to Grandpa Hymie. He said something to Grandpa like, "You're teaching him well." The street seemed to absorb all sound. Grandpa looked into the man's eyes, then bowed his head slightly. He took my hand, and gently led me away. We continued walking. I looked up into Peepop's face in my confusion and disappointment, and noticed tears in his eyes. Now even more confused, I said, "Grandpa, why are you crying? I gave the man my nickel." He bent near again, smiled gently, and replied, "I know, boychik, I know. These aren't tears of sorrow but joy. You created *pintale Torah, pintale yid*. You have a spark of goodness in your heart that you just gave to that man. Now he can take that spark and pass it on. That one spark can light thousands more." Then he continued in his soft lilting voice, saying, "You will always remember what you did today. You gave up something you wanted dearly." He grasped my little hand and finished with, "Come, boychik, we're going to the store to buy you some candy."

Grandpa Hymie was right; the moment, the story, and the lesson never left me. They're part of my heart.

* * *

8

Nickel Power

PASSING ON THE NICKEL

Forty-five years or so have passed since Peepop and I saw that crippled man. Nearly half a century since I dropped a nickel into his cup. For me, a lifetime. I'm a grown man, The Jewish Renaissance Family of Organizations is growing, and we are helping thousands of people every year in our community, around New Jersey and around the world. Grandpa Hymie's legacy stretches farther than he could ever imagine. Sometimes I wonder what he would say if he could come back for a day and look at his legacy in me. He might say, "Boychik, you remembered, didn't you?"

The story of the nickel does not actually end there in my memory of that Friday afternoon. Just as Grandpa said, one good action lights a spark in the heart of the recipient. Around 1999, an incident occurred

23

that brought Grandpa Hymie's statement back to me with force. I received a visit from a gentleman from Keasbey, New Jersey who told me he was employed as a janitor in a local school. As we chatted, he mentioned that he was accustomed to working hard to make a living. But he came to realize that hard work sometimes wasn't enough. It seemed that even though he was employed, the advent of summer presented him with problems. He wasn't scheduled to receive any salary until September, and he was having trouble making ends meet. This man had come to ask for help—never an easy thing to do. This hard-working fellow told me he had been all over asking for aid before he came to me. He had tried various times to access the funds he needed to keep his head above water, but he had failed. He related that he had been to Catholic Charities, to churches, and to the synagogues. One synagogue sent him to our offices. So it happened that he came to me.

He sat in a chair across from me as he told me his story. Then he asked me for a hundred dollars. He explained that with that amount, he would be able to pay his rent, stay in his home, and keep moving forward. My first inclination was to send him on his way. What if he just wanted the money for a good time? Then, my grandfather's face popped into my memory. I knew what he would do, so I handed the man the hundred dollars. I could see he was moved. "You don't know what this means to me. I won't have to move out of my home. I can pay my rent. I promise I'll pay this back to you in September when I get paid."

I stopped him and said, "This is what you can do for me. I don't want the money back. I want you to do the same thing I did for you; I want you to help somebody else. It doesn't have to be with money. I just want you to do something for somebody else, and when you do, I want you to let me know about it. Send an e-mail, or call me. Just let me know what you did."

He thanked me over and over, and then he left. I had really forgotten about the incident as time passed. About three months later, I received an e-mail from this gentleman. He said that his debt to me was paid. He explained that he had met a handicapped woman in the supermarket. While giving her a hand with her groceries, she told him her troubles. She leaned on her walker and confided to him that getting in and out of her home was dangerous and difficult. She needed a ramp to her door to increase her mobility and make her life easier. So he told me that he built the ramp for her. And, he added with emphasis, he refused to take any money for the job. He said, "I did what you said. I paid back my debt to you." I thanked him and told him that he had paid his debt twofold. I was deeply moved. But Grandpa's message wasn't over yet.

About a month later, the woman he had helped by building the ramp called me. She told me she found my number on the Foundation website. She related the story about the warmhearted and generous Good Samaritan who built her the ramp for her walker. This woman stressed that she was so thankful for what the man had done for her, that she did the same. She explained that she felt the need to pass this good-hearted gesture on as the man had done. She realized that she had a very particular skill that could help out sightless individuals: she could type Braille. So she decided to donate her time to a charity for the blind, transcribing books into Braille. She was planning to donate her time for the next six months to create printed material for the blind.

I thanked her, hung up the phone, and reflected on Grandpa Hymie's legacy. I thought about the road I was traveling, and meditated on my life—a life I believe was designed for me by the Almighty, and enacted here on earth by my family and me. I thought about what I had chosen to do with my life since closing the shoe store. Again, I was comfortable with my belief—my mission on earth is all about people helping people, and passing on that spark.

I know we are put on this planet to make a difference. We can forge positive changes. Each and every human being can make a life better for another. Even one person *can* make a difference that lights a spark in another man's heart. Each of us simply has to notice the need and find the way. When I look back to the day I dropped my nickel in the disabled man's pencil cup, and follow the path to this very moment, I see the path, and the lines connect.

THAT POWERFUL NICKEL

We had a terrible fire in Perth Amboy right around Christmas, 2010. Thirty-six townhomes in Harbor Town caught fire and burned. Thank G-d no one was seriously injured, but thirty-six families were displaced.

We reached out to everyone we knew to gather clothing, toys for the children, and money for security deposits and first month's rent on new living quarters. The city received a huge response from many sponsors and donors.

The Jewish Renaissance Foundation worked with the Red Cross, the city of Perth Amboy, other nonprofits and faith-based organizations. Even McGuire Air Force Base supplied food. We passed out food vouchers supplied by Pathmark and ShopRite supermarkets to the affected families, and helped find them lodging.

People were so generous that we had enough food and clothing for twice the number of families in need. We offered food and clothing to The Salvation Army's homeless shelter. That's where I met Bill (not his real name).

Bill was a homeless man who was sleeping at The Salvation Army. He was a very friendly gentleman who explained that he had just been released from the hospital after suffering a case of frostbite on his toes, due to a very cold winter. He had picked out a coat and a warm pair of boots. I offered him another coat, but he refused. He explained that, "These boots and coat are great. They fit perfectly. I really appreciate these things. But, I can only take what I can wear." And he thanked me.

Life on the street is very hard, even with assistance. The homeless who sleep at The Salvation Army must be out at seven each morning. Bill shared some additional thoughts with me. "Dr. G," he said, "I have everything I need right now. I can't carry too much, and since I'm staying at Salvation Army, it's still a bit difficult."

I told him to let me know if he needed anything else. He thanked me again, and we parted.

About a month later, I saw Bill at the Jewish Renaissance Medical Center.

"How're ya doing?" I asked. "How's everything going? How's your foot?"

"It's coming along; still a bit painful, but I'm doing much better. Again, thanks for the boots; they're keeping my feet lots warmer than the sneaks did! Right now, I just need to get some medications."

When I asked if he had funds for the medicines, he answered, "I'll make out."

I invited him upstairs to my office. I knew I had some money vouchers for our medical center's pharmacy. I asked him to sit down, and we chatted a bit. I was truly curious about this quiet man. We all have stereotypes in our minds when we think about homeless individuals. But many times our ideas are just that, stereotypes. They're all individuals, G-d's children, and I knew he had a story. I apologized in case he thought I was being too intrusive, but asked how he'd ended up on the streets.

He smiled and opened right up. "I had my own carpentry business, and it was going okay. But, I guess I was too nice a guy, because I was going ahead and finishing jobs when I hadn't been paid. My wife and I were having difficulties too, and we were about to divorce. So I had to move out of the house. I didn't have any ready money; there was just no money coming in. People weren't paying their debts to me. Basically, I found myself on the street. I was broke; my business was a goner. I was in a terrible place." He gave a little shrug and looked at me with a small smile.

I felt terrible for him. A series of bad breaks left him on the streets. He couldn't catch a break, but a break was exactly what he needed. So I asked, "Look, do you feel up to working part-time in our medical center's facilities department? Think you can handle it?"

My question brought a quick smile to his face. "Sure, sure, Dr. G." And he thanked me profusely.

"Come back in two days so I can get you all set up with the HR department."

The next day my staff weighed in. Their pre-judgments got the better of them. "What are you thinking? Are you crazy? This guy's homeless."

And I said, "This guy really touched my heart. Everybody needs a break, and this man is a prime example of that."

The staff slowly got on board with the idea of hiring Bill. Their reluctance was somewhat understandable. We had just had a sad and unfortunate experience with another employee. He had suffered some hard knocks and needed a hand. We gave him a part-time job, but after he had been with us about a year and a half, he became a problem. Some staff members thought he looked high. So we did what we were legally allowed to do, and tested him. Sure enough he was using drugs, so we had to let him go.

I wanted Bill to be upfront and truthful with me, so I outright asked him if he was on drugs or alcohol. He assured me he wasn't. He went through all the drug testing and background checks, and he came up clean. By the next week, he was on staff.

After a few months, the facilities director came to me to report that he was extremely satisfied with Bill. "I want to tell you something; you got a real gem here." At first I thought he was kidding around, but he added, "This Bill, he's unbelievable. He's a great guy. He follows directions like a pro. He's a talented carpenter, too. He can fix anything."

I was thrilled. So I asked the facilities director if he could use a full-time person on staff.

"If it's Bill, yeah."

So we made Bill a full-time employee.

He was still "living" at The Salvation Army. That meant he had very few possessions, including clothes. I gave him some more clothing and tried to supply whatever he needed to keep him going and help him get back on track. I also tried to mentor him. It continued to go great for Bill on the job. And now, he's been with us about two years.

Here's where the story gets even better. There's a woman named Rosa (not her real name) who was with one of our Workforce Investment Programs at the Jewish Renaissance Foundation. She moved up from the Workforce Investment Program into a full-time job at the medical center working in the facilities department. Rosa was a warm and friendly woman who got along well with everyone and was a terrific worker. To my surprise and delight, Bill and Rosa became engaged the following year.

Bill and Rosa are still working with us and continuing to prosper. Bill just got his driver's license back. I think he had some fines to pay off, but he's on track now. They're planning on getting an apartment together. All the parts of the plan are in place and they are moving forward. Like the nickel.

* * *

9

Yvonne Lopez's Comments

(FORMER CHAIRMAN, BOARD OF DIRECTORS, BOYS & GIRLS CLUBS OF PERTH AMBOY)

*A*lan is a very emotional person. His compassion and his emotions are so interlinked. They seep into one another. He drives and leads his life by compassion and by the passion of what he loves to do...and that's helping people. It's very simple; he thrives on helping others.

We all grow up with some kind of story. Alan sees beyond that. He sees the greatness in a person. The more difficult your life has been, the more compassionate he is. I find that extraordinary. Because in many cases when you're operating in business, you're always so careful to ensure that all the protocols are in place. For example, who you're hiring...that all the t's are crossed and the i's are dotted. Alan sees beyond all of that. He's always looking for the best in a person. He's very forgiving *that way. I find that to be an enormous quality in him. As a woman with decades of working, I have not come across many people like that.*

We had an applicant for a job who had difficult times in earlier years. This person came to us with a history of behaviors that a typical employer would look at and say, "Well, I'm not sure." Not Alan. Alan looks beyond that. Alan said, "This was fifteen, twenty years ago. We were all kids at one point and did stupid things. We all grow up. We all need an opportunity to show who we are as a person and to show our real worth in this world." I have to say, she's probably the hardest working employee that he has. This person valued…the fact that he took an interest, gave her the opportunity, and put faith and trust in her.

A week doesn't go by that I don't get a call from somebody wanting to work for the organization. I was on the phone for about twenty-five minutes with someone who was losing a job at the state level, a very high senior position, and he has been looking, watching our organization grow. The Jewish Renaissance Foundation is a growing, massive intelligent organization.

* * *

10

Becoming Alan Goldsmith

The Blessings in my Life:
1. My family
2. Playing football
3. Corvette accident
4. Shoe store
5. Networks of wonderful friends
6. Teaching
7. Starting a *yeshiva* (school)

My Beliefs:

1. I always believed that G-d was guiding me
2. Treat people the way you want to be treated
3. Laugh
4. Get the work done
5. Have a good time

* * *

11

Recollecting

My four grandparents—the Goldsmiths, and the Paleys—epitomized what a life of love, laughter, acceptance, tolerance, and tradition looked and felt like to a boy like me. These simple people escaped a life where hatred directed against them colored every moment of their days. Russia wasn't about to offer sanctuary to these Jewish peasants, their offspring, or their grandchildren. Their escape from a Russian *shtetl* (little town) brought them, ultimately, to Perth Amboy. By the beginning of the twentieth century, a Jewish community was developing there; they found a home they could relate to.

I have already recounted what I can remember from the family stories about my grandparents' escapes from Russia that led them to America. Today, when I look at photos of them taken when they were much younger than I am today, I try to imagine what life was like for them. I believe their eyes speak to me. It's as if I am able to see their honesty and openhearted-ness radiating from those photos. The values they held form my strong memories of these wonderful people. I sense what they must have felt as they approached this wonderful country with their hopes high and their expectations of democracy and fairness. They came here to find a place where they could live and raise children, without fear of torture and death. Practicing Judaism, love of family, love of others, and love of neighbors came naturally to these wonderful people. Those facts form the memories I hold so close to my heart.

Alan, 7 years old, with Grandma Sarah Goldsmith (left) and Grandma Ida Paley (right), 1954.

Mom, Dad, Alan's sister Dena (4 years), and Alan (8 years), 1955.

My mother, father, Dena (my sister), and I always shared meals, holidays, and spare time with all of them. I have joyous memories of my Grandpop Solomon and my Grandma Sarah. We spent many afternoons together in the small backyard of the two-family house on Madison Avenue. My father's parents lived upstairs, and we downstairs. I was only eight years old in 1955 when Grandpop passed away. I remember the confusion I felt when my father told me that Grandpop wouldn't be with us anymore; he had gone to heaven. His passing brought other changes to my young life. Dena and I began to spend more time with Grandpa Hymie and Grandma Ida. The main reason was because my father was now the one and only Goldsmith running the shoe store. Another big change was that my mother, out of necessity, went to work with him. I can honestly say that for some children, a setup like that might mean they were latchkey kids, but not for us. The Paley home was a second home to Dena and me. We adored spending time in their care. The aura around these two beloved grandparents was always tangibly loving and lighthearted.

No one liked a joke as much as Peepop and Grandma Ida. Humor and laughter were like the harmonies in the lilting family symphony they conducted. I remember my childhood in that environment being so comfortable, so warm, so easy, and so loving. Laughter and love were so intertwined, like notes of great music. My life still resonates with the tones of those melodies today.

* * *

12

Memorable Saturdays

I remember Saturdays with my grandparents, memorable moments that only bring me smiles. My mom and dad had to open the store on the Sabbath. People needed shoes, and my parents needed to work long hours to make a living, so the Saturday hours were a necessity. I wonder if in today's world a small family could live comfortably off the proceeds of one small neighborhood shoe store. But in the 1950s, it worked, and so did my parents. They worked very hard for us, but Dena and I didn't suffer in their absence. While they worked, we were well cared for. Sabbath rules were relaxed a bit at home for us, too. Time with Grandpa Hymie and Grandma Ida often revolved around the wonderful characters the brand new world of TV offered us.

Peepop and Grandma loved the programs and the stories as much as Dena and I did. Together, we watched Charlie Chan solve his mysteries, and

Hopalong Cassidy ride his white steed onto Grandpa's TV screen. The Lone Ranger and Tonto corralled the bad guys and rode off into the sunset to the pleasure of this little boy and his grandparents. We watched together, sharing high points and rejoicing together when the "bad guys" got their due.

Saturdays could just as easily find us playing cards. With my grandparents, this was another adventure altogether. Joking and laughing took almost as much time as dealing and playing. Peepop liked to cheat Grandma a little so he could gain the advantage; Grandma always let him. It was obvious and beautiful to watch them play the card game and their little game of delight with one another. Peepop would throw a card and try to take it back, while Grandma would laugh and challenge him with, "Oh, no you don't; you can't take it back." Once again, we were immersed in their love for us and each other. How we loved those games. How I loved those Saturdays.

Grandpa Hymie and Grandma Ida Paley in their backyard, Perth Amboy, 1958.

* * *

13

Jokes And Laughter

Wit and humor were part and parcel of my mother's personality, and my grandparents'. Our love had a jovial leitmotif that never failed us. Teasing was a way of life in and around our family. In fact, it still is. My mom, my Peepop, and I were all big teasers.

One wonderful story about a great joke relates directly to Grandpa Hymie. My grandparents lived with my parents during my college years. Dena had moved out prior to this, so they had her old room. I had arrived for a visit on a break from college. I was becoming a man and was about to show the family that I could hold my own in the teasing department. Grandpa Hymie always wore his hat; it was like he and that hat were connected. Setting up my great trick took some fancy maneuvering, because I needed to get my hands on the hat. I finally managed to get a hold of it when he put it down and wasn't looking. I stuffed the inside lining with toilet paper. When I say stuffed, I mean I *really* packed it. I wound toilet paper around and around, then refolded the lining to cover my handiwork. The job was unobtrusive; you could hardly see the bump. It was perfect. All I had to do was wait.

I told my mother and grandmother what I had done. They laughed, and they waited with me. We were like three criminals, hanging around the scene of the crime to see the whole story play out. We watched as Grandpa Hymie fiddled with his hat. It just didn't fit right. He kept saying that his hat was tight. He'd take it off, fiddle with it, and put it on. But it was still tight.

For three full days, he wore it that way. The hat just looked wrong; it sat a bit too high on his head, and he couldn't imagine why. We laughed and fooled around, and Peepop didn't know why.

On the third day, I finally admitted my dastardly deed to him. All the while he laughed and pretended to yell in anger. "Bandit (with the Yiddish inflection so it sounded like *Bondit*), I'm gonna get you, I'm gonna get you." How we laughed.

I was heading off to college. We were all preoccupied, and the house was bustling. I laid out my clothes for the trip. It was the next day that the "incident" took place.

I went out, probably to hang around with friends, say good-bye, that kind of thing. While I was out, my grandfather Hymie starched my underwear. He starched it board stiff, practically unbendable. Then he pinned the sleeves on my shirts and the pant legs. He pinned inside in a way that made them unwearable. He did a great invisible job. There was no way to see what he had done. This was the work of a pro. So the next morning, I got up early to get dressed for the long ride out to school in Missouri. I was understandably nervous, in a hurry to say my good-byes and hit the road. So I'm struggling with my shirts, my pants, my underwear. I couldn't get the pieces of clothing open to stick in my hand or leg. I couldn't unbend my shorts and T-shirts. What a wrestling match I had trying to put on my clothes. It was really early, and I was attempting to be quiet.

Then I heard him. Peepop peeked out of his room and started chuckling out there in the hall. We had a good laugh over that. He really "got" me. I laughed along with him and called him a bandit! That was the way it was in our home. I know I get my unending sense of humor from him.

What I didn't know, after sharing these heartwarming moments before returning to college to finish out the semester, was that I would never see Grandpa Hymie again. My beloved Peepop passed a few weeks later, just as I was about to take my finals. He was gone, but his legacy lives on.

I'm still a big tease, just like my grandfather. Add up the constant joking in my family to the locker room goofing around that I enjoyed with my good friends in sports, and it's easy to see how I became the joker that I am. It was a natural fit for me. But I do try to keep the joking under control.

* * *

14

Yvonne Lopez's Comments (2010)

Alan is a jolly guy. We had a board meeting a few weeks ago. You can't contain him; he's so jolly. "We're trying to have a board meeting here. What part of a board meeting don't you understand?" I said. (Laughing) "Please put that food away, that water away." He's just a jolly guy. We're conducting a board meeting, and Alan's conducting a side-bar conversation.

Alan feels good. You can see it in his walk, in his demeanor. He feels good about his contribution to society and to this world.

* * *

15
Driving—Of All Things

Who we are, the person each of us becomes, is formed by so many little items, tiny moments. Driving a car has never been my most polished skill. One story from my childhood comes to mind as I lead you toward a culminating moment in my life that, as you will see, also involves a car. But now I'm talking about my first experience with driving. I was a kid; I must have been thirteen, maybe fourteen. I remember feeling quite sure of myself at that age. I knew I could do anything I put my mind to.

My parents went on vacation in the dead of winter. I'm pretty sure they were headed off to a warm place. I stayed home with my grandparents. My father wanted me to start his car—just start it—so the battery wouldn't go dead. He had a great-looking sky-blue Chevy. I don't remember the model, but it was the year of long sleek bodies, with lots of chrome. The rear end was glorious, with the flared wings back there. It was a beauty, and I was so proud and excited to be given the responsibility to start Dad's car every day.

The first day, I fired it up. What a feeling for a young teenage boy. I could barely see out the windshield. I certainly couldn't see over the steering wheel. But as I sat in there, with heat pumping from the vents, feeling the power under my foot, I decided to move the car. So I scooted that huge car forward a bit.

The next day, I started it up and moved it back a few inches. It was thrilling. Now I really felt like I knew what I was doing. So, I pulled out of the parking space. I drove the car down the street. Here I was, peering *through* the steering wheel at the narrow street lined with parked cars on both sides. With a zoom, I took off. My ridiculous plan was to take Dad's car around the block and re-park it. Too bad I didn't take any contingencies into account; I just didn't see the problems. The street was extremely narrow, and there were cars parked along both curbs. What was required here was some very skillful maneuvering. In reality, that block was so tight, it really should have been a one-way.

I remember my fingers squeezing the life out of that steering wheel as I drove down the block, but my nerves and wishful thinking really didn't help. A car and a truck were sitting along the sides of the street. The car was a huge Desoto. This mammoth vehicle sat parked there, looking like a tank to my child's eyes. I must have grazed the side of that car and bounced against the bumper. I heard the bang that signaled my miscalculation. I gritted my teeth and steered up the block, around the corner, and finally parked Dad's Chevy.

I ran so fast into the house, while glancing behind me to watch for the police. I was sure they would be coming in a minute. Once inside, I kept looking out the front window of the house for the police to arrive. I was really scared.

Our upstairs neighbor asked what was wrong with my dad's car. First, it was parked near the middle of the street, and he mentioned that it looked like it had a huge dent in it. I nearly fainted. A dent! In my dad's car! I was a goner. The neighbor took the keys and went out to re-park the car. No sense leaving it hanging out in traffic. There was a large scrape on the side of my dad's beautiful Chevy, but not a scratch on the car I had bumped. I couldn't believe it. I was sure that the cops were going to knock on the door and pull me out of the house to confront the damage.

I was so terrified I didn't leave the house for three days. This fact did not escape my grandmother Ida, who was taking care of me. All I remember is the scene when my parents came home and my father saw what I had done to his beautiful car. He kept repeating, "My car, my car, my car…" Dad set out to punish me, but after he spoke to my grandmother, he said, "Grandma tells me that you punished yourself for three days by locking yourself in. Don't ever do anything like this again." And it was over. But my mishap with dad's car was, I believe, just a preview of my future car troubles.

* * *

16

Fonzie—Football—And Yarmulkes

High school was an exciting and fun time for me. I was a very typical kid. We had a "gang" (in the most harmless sense of the word). Most of us were Jewish in that bunch of kids. It just so happened that the Jewish gang hung out at the YMHA. But we had friends and teammates of every ethnicity, religion, and color. I can't really ever remember our having problems with classmates, teammates, or buddies because of those differences. Our similarities pulled us together, rather than our differences pushing us apart. We were schoolmates, jocks, friends. Our senior class president was black, and to us, that seemed a non-issue. Race wasn't part of our agenda. In fact, to me it seemed like we were living the *Happy Days* TV show in our own world right here in Perth Amboy.

Senior Class officers, Perth Amboy High School, 1966.
Alan was class vice-president.

When I think back, and I see how we were in high school, it's like I'm watching the New Jersey version of The Fonz and his friends. We were a close group; the football team was locked in friendship and sportsmanship. There really was no "I" in our team, but there was a lot of "we." In living out our version of a good teenage life, our rituals became another of our lassoes, another of the ties that bound us into the winning team we were. What a great group.

After the football games on Saturdays, we always went to Pamel's Sweet Shoppe at 129 Smith Street. It was the real-life version of the luncheonette found in today's reruns of TV shows from the 1950s and '60s. This was the typical drugstore you'd see in Norman Rockwell paintings, with a soda jerk behind the counter and high-necked shining siphons for the carbonated water that would make our Cokes, our root beer floats, and our egg creams. Absolutely everyone went there after the games for milk shakes and hamburgers. This was one of our traditions. And to sports-minded guys, on a sports-minded team, in a sports-minded school, our traditions were *very* important.

We raced to Pamel's for our important supply of milk shakes, sodas, and burgers. And we gathered there to just celebrate being young, I guess.

We were a tight bunch that had been playing together since freshman year, and we really stuck to our routines. We all fell into those habits not merely from enjoying them, but from a somewhat silly belief that our undefeated football success was such a miraculous thing that we were reluctant to change anything that was working for us on or off the field. So we stuck to our routines with a fervor only reserved for strong beliefs and superstitions.

Then there was Berlfein's Confectionary at 286 State Street. This was another gathering place for our gang, right in the middle of our town. We often went to Berlfein's after school, and I went in every Saturday morning before the football game for a cold orange drink and a Drake's Coffee Cake. This pre-game stop was crucial and eventually became the ritual for the whole team. We were a very superstitious bunch, so if something seemed to work, we were all for it. The whole team polished off that coffee cake and orange drink combo every Saturday during season.

Another of our traditions involved the *kippah*, the customary Jewish male head cover. I wore a *kippah*—also called a *yarmulke*—under my football helmet when we played. Our team was a mosaic, like our community, with blacks, whites, but with very little Hispanic presence in Perth Amboy in those years. Nonetheless, we were a mix of types and cultures, and we all got along just fine. So I wore my *yarmulke* under my helmet, and we played like pros. We had an undefeated season, thanks to good coaching, hard practices, good plays, and Drake's Coffee Cake.

Turned out everyone wanted a *yarmulke* for good luck, so after a while, everyone on the team wore one under his helmet. You can imagine how the cloth head coverings fared tucked up at the top of the helmet after hours and hours of sweaty practices, and then the hard-pumping action, game after game. Those *yarmulkes* were raunchy. But, once again, sports makes for great traditions, so neither the coach nor the players would touch them until the season ended. The whole season!

* * *

17

Ray Geneski's Comments

(ALAN'S FOOTBALL COACH, PERTH AMBOY HIGH SCHOOL, RETIRED)

When I think about the group of kids, what sticks out was how close-knit they were. They all hung around together off the field and away from training. Isn't that what every parent wants for his kid? For him to belong to a good group of friends? They were so committed to one another, and always got along. They could kid each other, they were always "on each other." The same way they played hard, they befriended each other. They gave no quarter on or off the field. An outstanding bunch of kids. Alan was one of them.

* * *

18

No Room For Racism

I remember one very important lesson I learned about racism. This one came directly from Grandma Ida (Paley). The Sabbath was our time with the grandparents. One particular Friday night, during dinner, the high school jock (that would be me) was busy recounting a joke heard somewhere at school or with friends. It was one of those stupid jokes about "Why can't somebody do something?" Screw in a light bulb, build a bridge, make ice…something ridiculous. And the answer had something to do with the person's ethnic group.

I was in the middle of enjoying the joke all over again, and laughing it up, when Grandma stopped me. This was Grandma Ida, who had about an eighth-grade education and spoke six languages. She became very upset and asked me how I would like it if someone told nasty jokes about a Jew. I agreed with her; I wouldn't like it at all. She told me how my telling these jokes about any group makes me less of a person. I hadn't realized how hateful those jokes really were. I felt terrible and ashamed. I said I would never tell another joke like that again. I stopped telling jokes that used ethnicity for a punch line. And now I always stop other people if they try to tell me one. Jokes about other races and religions stopped being funny right there at Grandma's table.

* * *

19

Grandparents Redux

*I*n a beautifully recursive manner, my retelling comes back again and again to the deep and strong foundation set by my grandparents, the pillars of my existence. My life is simply a thick, rich, warm tapestry woven from the beautiful stories and examples my grandparents and parents told and lived. As the weavers of my story, in creating this beautiful tapestry as a legacy for me, those six wonderful people continually added ideas, examples, and laughter to form the warp and weave of this cloth. Many of those shining threads were in the form of stories. My grandparents always told me stories.

Many of those tales related to the teachings and allegories from the Bible. So the fact that I always related my football career to the small boy David in his victory over Goliath is not surprising. Grandpa Hymie told me that story again and again. I always remembered it. If someone knocked me down or beat me on the football field, I looked at that moment as one skirmish in a longer battle. The moment may have been lost, I may have been knocked over, but the loss was only a momentary setback in the whole war. I knew I could come back from defeat. I knew I could out-think my opponents. I knew I was quicker than my adversaries. I always pushed forward, strong in my convictions. Convictions that were delivered to me by my parents and grandparents. Their stories, their strong beliefs, and their love nourished that core in me.

* * *

20

"The Boys"

School was never my main focus; various sports were. But I wasn't always the strong guy I became in high school. When I was in fifth grade, I contracted measles and then pneumonia and was in bed for nearly six months. I had never been so sick before. I missed a good part of the school year. Out of necessity, I had to repeat a grade. By that time (1955) my Grandpop Solomon had passed away. By anyone's standards, he had been too young to go; he was only fifty-five when we lost him that year. Now my father ran the shoe store with my mother's help.

I don't think people realize how much time and effort it takes to keep a small business running. They devoted long hours to our livelihood. If the store wasn't open, my dad couldn't sell shoes. So, a six-day week was standard for my parents. They could devote this time to dad's shoe store, because they knew we were well looked after by our grandparents.

Dena and I spent wonderful long hours with Grandma and Grandpa Paley during this extended time when I was so sick. I remember the laughter in their home. Once I was well, there were other changes for us. We moved out of the two-family house. Grandma Sarah stayed in the upstairs unit, and my future wife's grandmother moved downstairs, Bubbe Cohen. We, of course, had no idea of that future connection, but looking back, it just underscores the small-town nature of this great little town. In the fifties, Perth Amboy still resembled a new-world *shtetl*.

This was not an easy time for me. Making friends for an eleven- or twelve-year-old boy never is, especially after having missed so much time from school and being held back one full grade. All my friends were now a grade ahead of me, and had now moved on to sixth grade in the middle school. Losing my friends was difficult. Yet, I did make friends, and found my place in a new group.

I had some good friends who lived near me, Michael Myerwitz, Morton Rosenberg ("Morty"), and Danny Kaden among them. We formed part of a group of friends, largely Jewish, who had developed a tight bond. In fact, we called ourselves "The Boys." Thinking about it now, we were kind of like the kids in that movie *The Sandlot*. We were tight; we did everything together. Life was great. We were from the same neighborhood and enjoyed YMHA activities together. One incident that stands out related to one of my life pillars—sports.

I practiced judo at the YMHA. I can't remember why I chose this discipline. But I spent many, many hours during my junior year in high school with this sport, working to perfect my form and timing. I was pretty good. In fact, the summer before my senior year, I achieved brown-belt status and won the state championship in my weight class. But that came later.

I guess I was always the strongest of my friends; I tended to protect the other kids. One time, when we were in seventh or eighth grade, a bully—a really big kid around seventeen or eighteen years old—was picking on us. I can't think of a reason why this kid had it in for us, but the nature of the bully brought him to us.

This one time, this huge kid grabbed a hat from one of my friends. My immediate instinct was to grab it back, just like that. I snatched it from this immense kid's grasp, and the thought zipped into my mind, "What did I just do?" I mean, this kid was *really* big. I gave the hat back to my friend, and now, it seemed, I was going to have to fight. This kid really wanted to go at it. He swung, and I, gathering all my instincts from judo, took him down.

The discipline of judo taught us not to fight, so I just stopped him cold and held him down. I saw teachers walking around and wondered why none of them came to help. I didn't want to fight this kid. I kept him on the ground until finally a teacher came by and broke it up. I was so relieved to see that teacher. I didn't do this for any reason other than to prevent a fight. I didn't want attention, but the kids kind of set me up as a hero all afternoon.

Adulation wasn't what I wanted, and I certainly didn't want a fight. I didn't want an escalation of this silly incident, but I found out that this big kid had a knife and was going to wait for me after school.

I always had a way with words, and being the fast-talker that I am, I started regaling him with my point of view as soon as I saw him that afternoon. I explained to him why we shouldn't be fighting. "Yeah, I scraped you up, you scraped me up," I said, "but we shouldn't be carrying on any longer." I must have said something right, because my words pacified him.

Later on, I found out that this kid had been afraid of me and felt that he had to save face. Again, when I look back at this, I see one of the stepping stones on my path. I guess when it comes to protecting and watching over people, especially my friends, I am there. I have always done that. In our case, our little group of pals was safe; no one picked on us after that.

The path that brought me to the Jewish Renaissance Foundation and the world of need is full of friends. I can't stress enough the importance and impact that sports have had on me, my world, and my pathway. Most of us were jocks in high school. Michael Myerwitz was a really good track star and basketball player. It was as if we gravitated toward the actions and activities that created closeness and straight living. We all played sports.

Through high school I was always active. I lifted weights; I loved what it did for me and how it made me feel. In those years lifting wasn't as popular and widespread as it is today. In fact, weight lifting was way outside the mainstream. Charles Atlas advertised his weight lifting courses in comic books! It was not a commonplace gym activity like it is today. But, for some reason, I really enjoyed it.

I also participated in three letter sports. I practiced indoor track and outdoor track, and learned to throw javelin. I tried wrestling, but didn't really like that as much as the others. What healthy lives we lived through and with our sports and our friendships.

And then there was football.

* * *

21

Ray Geneski's Comments

Alan and Jay Ziznewski played together in high school. They looked like Mutt and Jeff. Jay's six-foot-eight towered over Alan's five-foot-six, so they were a sight together. Jay watched out for Alan. He was the detail man in all of what Alan had created. They've been best friends since high school football.

I don't know what there is about sports. You develop a togetherness from playing team sports. You play with a bunch of guys, and these friendships are enduring, genuine, and everlasting. These two are prime examples of that kind of friendship. I used to tell them, "If you have two or three good friends in your whole life, you're lucky. If you have five, you're sitting on top of the world." Close friends are hard to come by. One great way to make them is to work together for a common cause; that's what these kids did. That's what they're still doing.

* * *

22

In The Land Of Giants

*P*icture me on the high school football team...all five-foot-six of me, a height-challenged jock among giants. Compare this to today's defensive walls, built of six-foot (and taller) blocks of humanity. I was nowhere near the tallest guy on our team and surely not bigger than our opponents. Five-six, but strong.

The long and the short of the Perth Amboy High School football team. Jay Ziznewski and Alan Goldsmith, 1965. Today Jay serves as the Jewish Renaissance Family of Organization's lawyer.

All those years practicing judo at the "Y" and lifting weights had filled me out and given me strength. I always worked out, striving for physical strength and endurance. I was a fighter, but not in the bullying way. I was the short guy joining the football team and winning, against the odds.

I was also the only Jewish player on the team at that time. We had a great team; we pushed hard, played strong, and worked tightly. The team became conference champs, and I became "All County." The only way I can explain this accomplishment is to see myself akin to David from the biblical story. Against the odds, that little guy stood up to a giant and beat him. Knocked him right down. But all through his life, his leadership, stamina, and courage helped guide and lead him to becoming one of the most famous and well-loved kings of all of them. So the story of David and Goliath fits the bill for me as a beacon, and as another of the stepping stones on the guiding path of my life.

* * *

23

Ray Geneski's Comments

igh school football. That's where my relationship with Alan started. On the field, in the locker room. I was, let's see, in my thirties, somewhere around that age, when I first met the fire-plug named Alan Goldsmith. After all, Alan is about five-foot-six. I can't even imagine a guy that size going out for football today. But back then, he became an important part of our team.

He was in great physical shape. He always participated in sports, worked out, took care of himself. Maybe that's because of the type of person he is. Once he put his mind to something, he worked and worked and got it right. It's not really a game that runs in the blood of Jewish kids; in fact, Alan was one of the few Jewish foot-ball players we ever had on our high school team.

He was a kid from a different era. When you compare those years, the type of children we coached then, you can notice the difference. The kids back in the '60s were well brought up. They were taught respect and honesty and all the values that their parents believed in. Those were the values transmitted to their children, and we noticed it in the school.

I think I first met Alan when he was a high school freshman. I remember the first time I saw him. I was then the assistant varsity coach. I had gone over to watch the freshmen practice. I saw this squat kid, you know a little short, well-built, stocky, playing fullback. I watched him run the ball one time, and I said to his coach, "Now he's a guard. No more fullback." Yeah, that was the first time. I coached him for three years, sophomore, junior, and senior years. Then he left Perth Amboy and went to college.

Let me tell you, this group of kids, the ones I coached with Alan, they were a good bunch of kids. He was one of a great gang. He and his teammates were all dedicated to the game. A clean-cut bunch, they made my job more inviting and worthwhile. Alan played well for us; he was a good player. We had a pretty good team then. These kids were dedicated to one another and to the cause...to winning.

As their coach I would never tell them they were any good. I would always tell them they could be better.

* * *

24

John Wayne
And College

My high school football prowess and power moved me forward on the field and also in my life. I was like a lot of other jocks, for whom football became the tool, the engine in our lives that helped to propel us toward our goals. Some of these goals were fixed in our minds and our visions, but others were invisible. Those unseeable goals only became noticeable as our lives progressed and our talents developed.

After high school I received two scholarship offers, one to Fork Union Military Academy and one to Tarkio College in Tarkio, Missouri. A peach of a life awaited me. My college years loomed in front of me, the halls of academe, football, books, and ideas, football, fraternity life, football, and new friends, and of course, football. But I had other plans. I was just a young kid (but if you had said that to me at that time, I would have argued to the contrary.) I was an idealist then as I suppose I am now. My visions of doing the right thing didn't just pop out of nowhere.

High school graduation, at home in Perth Amboy with mom and dad, 1966.

So in 1966 when I was preparing to embark on my post-high school life, dreams of doing right by the world began growing in my imagination. I started dreaming up a noble and altruistic vision of myself as a defender of democracy. I was headstrong and, like many young men of the time, I thought I knew my head and my heart.

The conflict in Vietnam was growing in scope and importance for our country, and I was pretty set on joining the army. I saw myself defending my wonderful homeland, helping out with might for right, and then returning home to move on. In this dream vision of my life, I pushed college back a few years. I felt I had something else to do before I continued studying.

To the best of my recollection, I think I had just seen *The Green Berets*, John Wayne at his best. He was a huge role model for an impressionable young guy like me. Of course, I was influenced. I had a friend, Eddie Andryszczyk, a ball player who felt the same way. Powerful stuff to a young man with visions. We decided that we could achieve great things like

Wayne, by joining the Green Berets. Football, war...it all seemed like the same thing to us. Just like the game, all we had to do was make a plan, execute the play, and win.

My father had other ideas. My dad, who had never gotten physical with me in my entire life, actually grabbed me by the ear. He pulled my ear, sat me down, and told me in emphatic terms and language that I was not joining the Green Berets, that I was not enlisting in the army, and I was not shipping off to war. Dad, it turned out, was bigger and stronger than John Wayne.

My father had served in World War II. He actually served in what was the last cavalry unit, with horses and everything. He spent time overseas, saw the worst of war, and eventually received a transfer into a medical supplies unit. World War II raged, and he was in the thick of it. I couldn't imagine then how it had shaped his view of the world. He had been preparing to ship out to Japan when the war ended. He had spent time in Africa, saw combat, and knew more about war than he ever wanted me to know.

So, when he finally let go of my aching ear, he announced that he would not allow me to join the army; he wanted to see me in college. There was no way I could disobey my father. Of course I listened to him. I knew he was serious. I got in step with his marching orders. I knew my parents would do whatever it took, and give all they could muster, to see me through a college education. So, I accepted admittance at Tarkio, a small Presbyterian school in Missouri.

I liked Tarkio. I was out in the Midwest, which was such a huge change from the East Coast. At Tarkio, I was a person, not a number. I was able to bring a bit of home with me. It was as if the neighborhood feeling I had growing up in Perth Amboy followed me to college. I started as a music major, but music really wasn't my strong suit. I loved music, always have, and played a little piano, some guitar, and the accordion. But I never felt that I was terribly good.

One story about my musical talent (or lack thereof) always gives me a chuckle. There was a professor at Tarkio, a little Italian guy who, unfortunately, would agree with that statement about my lack of talent. I remember a fateful and not terribly great piano recital of mine at college.

I was at the piano in front of a room full of people. I was prepared to hammer out my best version of Beethoven's "Moonlight Sonata." I began banging out the piece when my brain went blank. My fingers somehow kept moving, knocking out some type of music, and I continued at the piano for long minutes. I realized I was at a total loss, so, with a flourish, I pounded out a cadence (a finishing series of notes). Then, I stood up, bowed, bowed again, and walked off, only to hear the professor groan, "My reputation...my reputation is ruined!" I never knew if he was kidding or not, but as I left the stage to raucous laughter and applause from my fraternity brothers, I really knew that music wasn't meant to be part of my life's path.

That knowledge hit home after tryouts for the choir trip to Europe that ended with the choir director pulling me aside and telling me, "Goldy (my nickname), you have two options: mouth the words silently and go on tour with us, or quit." I really wanted to go to Europe, so I took the first option. I toured with the group, and had a grand old time. I wouldn't have wanted to miss out on that wonderful experience. But I was no dummy; I quit the music major the following year. Then I tried an accounting/business major, but that wasn't the right fit for me either. My idea of balancing the books was never in sync with the professor's. Sports, once again, was the key. What really attracted me was physical education, and that became my major.

* * *

25

Tom Devlin's Comments

(PHD, SUPT.OF SCHOOLS, FT. LEAVENWORTH,
RETIRED)

*I*t was 1966, my freshman year at Tarkio. In August Alan and I both arrived to attend football camp as Tarkio College freshmen. We were both starters on the team. It just so happens that Alan and I were put together as roommates in the athlete's dorm. So I met him sometime in August of '66 when I walked into the dorm room at Tarkio.

So we spent numerous years together playing football at Tarkio College. We were also members of the same fraternity, Psi Lambda Phi, and enjoyed a pretty robust social calendar during our college years. Goldy was Goldy—he was a presence among anybody, any group of people. He kind of stood out with his engaging personality…always a smile on his face…he had a quick wit about him.

Alan was part of a wonderful family. I met his mom and his dad way back then, and of course his sister Dena. I spent time at their house as Alan did at mine. I was one of the best men at his wedding and he at mine. As a matter of fact, he is the Jewish godfather to my Catholic daughter.

* * *

26

Sports At Tarkio

I played football and participated in track and field at Tarkio College all four years. Tarkio was a very small school, about 800 students. In fact, I think Tarkio was the smallest college in its division.

Sports was and is one of the keys to my life. I was always part of a winning team, and I love remembering that feeling. I always had the will to win. And, with each team I joined, I became a brother to a wonderful group of guys. A team is such a powerful force. I felt it way back then. Years later, with the certainty I have acquired from life experience, I am still firm in the knowledge that sports is a part of me, of who I am.

As an athlete, I found myself striving to do something hard. The goal was there in front of me…goalposts standing tall into the sky, points to add to our score, a touchdown. I spent so much time striving with and toward a goal that had been set out, defined, and visible. I always knew that it was going to take a lot of punishing work and physical activity and pain. But I always knew that I could get to the goal…if I worked hard enough.

This was the basis for the rest of my life. When I look back, I see the road lined with the rewards that, directly and indirectly, sports have delivered to me. My thoughts and memories of sports form a big part of the pathway that ultimately led me to the Foundation.

Tarkio College football (Tarkio, Missouri), 1968. Alan (62) standing next to Tom Devlin (80), college roommate who became a life-long friend.

* * *

27

Tom Devlin's Comments

I remember one particular football game. Tarkio was playing Doane College at the time. Doane's team was an unbelievable powerhouse. They were in our conference, but they were also ranked nationally. They were having an undefeated season up to that point. I remember this one game. We were trying very hard to win. Goldy and I were both on the kickoff receive team, and of course we were there to throw blocks and stop anyone in any way we could...so our ball carriers were free to run. I had thrown a block and rolled off and saw a leg. So I just grabbed the leg and held on, thinking it was one of the defensive guys ...and I hear someone yelling and screaming at me. When I looked up, I saw that I had a vise grip on Goldy. I was holding him back from making a block or whatever he was trying to do. I was just trying to make as many blocks as I could, trying to make a difference.

Football creates a brotherhood. You travel together, you work together, you play together, and you have fun together. With Goldy, I guess we both have that kind of easygoing personality, because neither one of us takes himself too seriously. We tend to laugh a lot. My wife knows Goldy really well, and between the three of us, it's still usually a fun fest when we're together. My wife and I both love him. He's more than just a friend to us; he's family.

We were both young, and energetic, and athletic. Goldy and I played football together there at Tarkio College. We were starters on the football team and played all four years. Alan is Alan, I don't know how to describe him as other than fun-loving, very kind, with a magnetic type of a personality. I don't know anybody who has ever been around him who didn't totally enjoy his presence or his way of being.

We've known each other since 1966; that's over forty years of a very good relationship between good friends. Although he's living in New Jersey and I'm retired and living in Florida, he certainly keeps in touch with me and I with him. I flew back when they honored him and presented him with his IIMSAM (United Nations) credentials with a banquet. My wife and I returned to New Jersey, spent a little time with Alan and Ann, and attended the function, which was wonderfully done and deservedly so for Alan.

* * *

28

College Graduate

I graduated from Tarkio in 1970. The times were conflictive. Society was still in great turmoil. The furor in our country over the war was growing; the Vietnam War was still raging. Like most young guys, I had to appear for my physical. I didn't have the burning desire to fight that had consumed me four years earlier.

It really was a crazy time in America. Guys were running for the Canadian border and doing outlandish things to stay out of the service. Young men were going to great lengths by that time to win deferments of any kind. In fact they were zooming past all the limits of normal to win those deferments. Guys who went for their physicals were climbing on tables to act crazy, urinating in their pants, and generally acting like nuts to get some kind of pass on this war. I brought old x-rays with me, counting on all those football injuries to keep me out of Vietnam. I passed my physical in spite of all those injuries, and was deemed able to serve. But my father's words from years before weighed heavily on me. I wanted to serve my country, and yet felt I couldn't go against his strong desires.

* * *

29

The Peace Corps

A natural choice for me was the Peace Corps. I could still serve my country in a way with which I was comfortable and it didn't countermand my father's desires. This was the first year of the draft lottery. It's funny the things I remember, like my lottery number. I was number 213, and it seemed a good bet that I could be drafted. As it turned out, my number wasn't called. That year, they only got to number 197. However, my mind was pretty much made up.

I still chose to enter the Peace Corps. I felt a need to serve America, and this was a great way to do it. What an exhilarating feeling it was for me to join this group. I was in a position to learn about new cultures, new people, new ways of life. A huge benefit was that I learned to speak Spanish. They brought us into San Ysidro, California, near Tijuana, Mexico. We really learned to fend for ourselves there.

I stayed with a very lovely Mexican family. I believe their name was Cedillas. They took me in like I was one of their own. There were three young guys in that home, one son named Pedro, me, and another young man. We were so lucky to live with this wonderful family. They fit us right into their routines, and we started picking up all kinds of new and interesting knowledge from them. We learned their language, customs, and culture. Pedro introduced us to all facets of life in and around that little town. I was getting set to be a teacher trainer, and headed to Venezuela to begin serving.

In the Peace Corps, Alan teaching volleyball to a group of girls, Isla de Margarita, Venezuela, 1970.

Peace Corps, enjoying a barbecue with other volunteers during Carnaval, 1971.

Almost like a preview of my far distant future, we met with the president of Venezuela, in Caracas. What a thrill that was. Then I was sent to the Isla de Margarita. I was there to train teachers how to better serve the needs of their students. So off to school it was. With my training, I helped those inexperienced educators set goals and guide those kids. It was a tremendously rewarding time filled with so many new people and experiences.

I spent nearly two years in that country, helping the educators and their pupils while I mastered Spanish. When my time there ended, I was at loose ends. I found myself back home, not really knowing what I wanted to do.

Perth Amboy was changing. Like so many New Jersey cities with a small-town feeling, my hometown was experiencing new currents. Those friendly little neighborhoods I remembered were losing people to the suburbs. So many familiar families were leaving. Along with the migration of individuals was the loss of the small businesses that lined the streets of downtown. The families that owned and worked in them moved on. The ability of this town to sustain those businesses had diminished. The shopping malls in the suburbs were rising and pulling the business centers out of the older cities. By this time, the mid- '60s and early '70s, change had come to Perth Amboy in a big way. Along I came, with no plans, into a city changing even faster than I could imagine.

* * *

30
Grad School

Graduate school became my target on my return from the Peace Corps in 1972. With graduate school in my sights, coaching became the bulls-eye. I gravitated to the Midwest again, and ended up at Northwest State Missouri University, very close to my alma mater, Tarkio College. So I coached football with my old coach at Tarkio—Coach Lade—and studied for a masters degree in health and physical education. That worked out well for me. My alma mater offered me the credits I needed to become a teacher. They credited me for all the teacher training I had carried out in the Peace Corps. Because I didn't have a teaching certificate, they gave me the credits toward earning one. I completed student teaching there in Missouri to earn that certificate.

In 1972, Alan assistant coached the Tarkio College football team while studying for a Master's Degree at N.W. Missouri State University.

* * *

31

Tom Devlin's Comments

*A*lan went to the Peace Corps after college, served in South America, and then came back. I helped him get enrolled in graduate school. I was living and teaching in Tarkio, Missouri at the time. I had moved right from my bachelor's degree into my master's degree program. I was enrolled at Northwest State Missouri University, and went over and got Alan enrolled. Carla and I had married as seniors while we were still studying at Tarkio. Goldy stayed with us for a couple of days until I got him a roommate and a place to stay. And he went on to graduate school at Northwest State Missouri. He graduated with his master's degree; I believe it was in physical education. (laughing) I'd like to remember that I got my PhD before Alan got his.

* * *

32

Back Home

By 1973, I was an accredited teacher searching for a job. I applied to schools in different areas, but decided to come back to Perth Amboy. The pull of my hometown was tremendous. I loved the memories that filled me. Everybody knew me, knew my family. I interviewed with the assistant superintendent, who told me, "Goldy, you're the one we want!" I was offered a job teaching middle school. Not only did they know me, but I was coming home to coach the high school football team I loved. As a bonus, I was now bilingual...and our town was now about 50 percent Latino. They knew me there...they knew my high school football record... they knew of my coaching at the college level, and I was home. I was now a Perth Amboy teacher!

* * *

33

Ray Geneski's Comments

W hen Alan came back to Perth Amboy after graduate school, he came
back to teach. He started in the middle school, then came over to the
high school. I had become head coach by then and Alan coached with
me for a year. Then, I think it was around 1980, he left teaching to go into his
father's shoe business.

When he left to take over his father's business, his father either wasn't well or
had just passed away. Alan ran the business until 1996 and started the Jewish
Renaissance Foundation in the back room of the shoe store. That was a pretty amazing time. His grandfather had opened that store. Goldsmith Shoes was an institution in Perth Amboy. Most of the stores back then were family-owned, mom-and-pop
type of operations. Goldsmith's was in business for years and years. Most of those

businesses ran for seventy-five, maybe a hundred years, something like that. There aren't many anymore. You know how it goes, the kids go off to college, go their own way, maybe they're doctors, businessmen, lawyers, what have you. The kids left; the mom-and-pop stores died out.

* * *

34

Perth Amboy — All Grown Up

Coming back to the city of my birth, my childhood, and my school years was quite an occurrence. Anyone can imagine what it's like, returning, grown to adulthood, but re-entering the world of your youth. So many of the people I grew up with had moved on, but there was a core of people, friends, with whom I re-established contact. This was the time period when I met Ann, my future wife.

* * *

35

My Derech Hashem—My Path

*T*he Bible and the teachings of Judaism were a foundation for the Goldsmith family. My four grandparents made it so. Tied to the influence the Bible stories had on me is the certainty and assurance I have always felt with regard to my destiny.

I have always believed that there was a hand guiding me on the pathway to my life, a force that knew the answers and wouldn't let me stray. I believe I am traveling a *Derech Hashem*, G-d's path to follow. The Almighty has laid out the way for me. I think I knew even when I was very young that every one of my steps was purposeful. The Almighty gave me physical strength and athletic prowess. He gave me parents and grandparents who were loving, forthright, honest, and decent people. The hardworking legacy I inherited from them and the strong sense of integrity have never failed me. What I learned at the side of my dad in the family shoe store served me well as a shoe salesman, and beyond.

I know that I did not only learn to be a salesman to sell shoes, but to sell ideas. My ability to sell the ideas that made the Jewish Renaissance Foundation a reality and brought us to the point we're at today, helping people in New Jersey and around the world, is nothing short of a miracle. What my father and grandfathers taught me has served me equally well as president of the Jewish Renaissance Foundation, in negotiations with politicians and bankers, dealing with the United Nations ambassador to Hungary, or speaking to gatherings at the U.N. as Goodwill Ambassador to IIMSAM. What I do, what I learned, and who I am are directly related to whom G-d made me, and to the family of wonderful, honest, loving men and women he provided for me.

* * *

36

Woman Of
My Dreams

*T*he summer I finished my master's degree, 1972, was the summer of the dream. Before I can describe meeting Annie, my wonderful wife, I need to talk about The Dream. I have already mentioned that I believe my life is guided. I know with certainty that I live under G-d's guiding hand. I have had this feeling for most of my life. It gives me a certainty about what I am doing and where I am headed. And then I had The Dream.

I dream a lot, and usually remember them. This dream was different in a special way. It was especially vivid and impressed me to a point that I have never forgotten. This particular dream has become another moment in my life that needs to be documented in order to explain my journey.

Even then I paid attention to The Dream because it seemed so out of the ordinary, so crazy. In that dream, I found myself near a lake. It was very big, seemed very deep, a lovely spot. A woman appeared near the lake. She was totally dressed in white, a woman so beautiful that she seemed to be of another world. Her beauty surpassed that of every other woman on earth. I was astounded and actually besotted with this gorgeous creature. I fell in love with this dream woman. I wanted to spend time with her and get to know her. Even though I woke up to reality, this dream and that woman had made a huge impact on me. I had no idea what this dream meant.

That summer, back in Perth Amboy, with my master's degree tucked into my bag of tricks, I embarked on a new part of my life. I had the whole summer in front of me before I was to begin teaching and coaching in the Perth Amboy public schools. I went to work with my dad in the shoe store. He and I spent day after day of my summer vacation working side by side. He started teaching me about the shoe business. I liked that, and I loved spending time with him. Dad's store was *the* neighborhood shoe store, so sooner or later, everyone from the nearby streets and communities passed through our shop.

The clientele in those days consisted of the older generation of people who had "grown up" with the Goldsmith Shoe Store. These were the men and women of my parents' generation from the neighborhood. One of the clients was a woman I called "The Butcher's Wife." Her husband was the neighborhood kosher butcher, and her name was Ida Shechter. She and I chatted, and she gossiped with my dad. In short, we knew her, and she knew us.

The way I remember the event was that my dad was waiting on Ida, my future mother-in-law, one day. I was doing something nearby. I don't know what I was involved with, but I was close enough for Ida to grab me. She gave me one of those "mother looks" and said, "Why don't you ask my daughter out on a date?" Boy, was I cornered. She had hit me with the ubiquitous question of all mothers for all time. I knew who her daughter was. In a town like Perth Amboy, you basically knew everyone by sight, even if they weren't among your circle of friends. Her daughter, Ann, had been in a class one year ahead of me.

Ann was gorgeous. I mean she broke the beautiful scale. In fact, she was the most beautiful woman you'd ever want to see. She actually looked like Elizabeth Taylor. Ida gave me her telephone number, and I set up a date.

I'd like to say, "And the rest is history," but it wasn't that simple. I took Ann on a date, but I wasn't planning on asking her out again. Chalk it up to my youth, lack of experience, and every other quirk that besets young men. Don't get me wrong, I thought she was great. I just wasn't in a hurry to date Ann or anyone else. I wasn't in any hurry to make commitments, not even dating commitments.

However, I did ask her out again. And again. I wasn't sure if she was "the one" for me. But we kept going out; we kept learning about one another. As I got to know Ann Shechter, I began to see in her the qualities I wanted in the woman who would be my wife. She and her parents lived a block from Grandpa Hymie and Grandma Ida, which means she grew up a block from where I lived as a child. She graduated from the same high school I did. So many facts and facets of our lives were tied together by geography and happenstance. It was like we came from the same *shtetl*. I began to have a feeling that this relationship was being arranged from Heaven.

A year later I proposed to Ann. As I remember it, she couldn't make up her mind.

Since Ann couldn't decide whether or not to marry me, Ida jumped in to help. She told her daughter, "This is the man you want to marry." I've always been glad she helped Annie make that decision.

Remembering that crazy dream, and connecting it inextricably to Annie made me feel like all I had to do was put one and one together to get two. We were brought together by the hand that has led me all my life. From Above came the guidance. No luck involved.

* * *

37

Ann Goldsmith's Comments

When I was celebrating my thirty-eighth birthday, Alan set up a surprise party for me. He designed an invitation and used an old photo from our early years. The picture was taken in Hebrew school. We were in class together as very young children. There we stood in that black and white image, shoulder to shoulder. But we had no idea of each other's existence. We lived in the same town growing up, but didn't really hang out in the same groups of friends.

Alan (rear, left) performing a Chanukah song with classmates at Hebrew School, 1957. Unbeknownst to Alan, he is standing next to his future wife, Annie.

I am younger than Alan, but I was a year ahead of him in school. I knew of his family; I knew his sister. If somebody told me his name, I could picture who he was. But in all the years we were growing up, I really never knew him. Here's a funny thing, and shows just what a small village Perth Amboy was when we were kids: the neighborhoods were like little villages. My grandmother lived in a two-family house that was owned by Alan's grandmother (Goldsmith). So our families were connected by geography and the daily interactions of Jewish life in our town.

The year Alan returned home, after his stint in the Peace Corps and his master's degree, he was in a situation trying to decide what to do. He got a job as a phys ed teacher. But he was always associated with his father's business. He spent time there working alongside his dad even after he took the teaching position. That's where our paths crossed again.

My parents shopped in his father's store. They knew the Goldsmiths; they knew of their son. So my mother and his parents chatted, about their children surely, and one thing led to another. I can hear them now: "My daughter this, and my son that." So between the parents, they thought up this idea for Alan to ask me out on a date. We were very different people. He was the jock, the football player; I was the studious person. And as I said, I never really knew him when we were in high school.

So this jock calls me up and asks me out. I will never forget this. We wound up at the Pancake House. It happened to be Passover week, and because of that I could not eat anything served at this restaurant, and there is my date, eating for the two of us. I do remember that Alan told me he was not going to call me again.

I was showing dogs way back then. After that first date, I didn't think much about Alan, but as things worked out, we crossed paths again. I was going to a dog show, and the person I had hired to help out couldn't make it. This person was supposed to help with the crates and equipment. I couldn't manage it myself. So I called Alan and said, "Hi, have you ever been to a dog show?" He said no. So I said, "Would you like to take a ride with me and see what it's all about? I could really use some help; I need some strong hands to lug all the equipment." Alan came along; after that we continued dating.

From the summer into the fall, we dated. I remember it being, at most, half a year. He announced to me that he wanted to get married. I remember walking into my parents' house that day crying. It was a very emotional moment for me.

Alan was a phys ed teacher and I was an elementary teacher when we married. He was coaching football and tennis at the high school. Even though he was busy, after football season, he would go into his father's store on Saturdays to help him, to lend a hand.

I remember that he was also working on his dissertation. I can't count the hours I spent with him at Rutgers, helping him with his papers. The amount of work we put in on that was huge. Sometimes I joke that I should have gotten the degree along with Alan.

* * *

38

The Shekhinah

(MY GUIDE, MY SALVATION)

*I*n Jewish lore, the Bible relates the story of Moses leading the Jewish people out of Egypt. They wandered in the desert for forty years under the *Shekhinah*. The *Shekhinah* was the cloud of glory that always led the Israelites through the desert and protected them. The *Shekhinah* was their protection, their guide, their guard, their shield. I am always reminded of that story. I have come to believe that I too live under a *Shekhinah*. I have been protected and watched over by a power far greater than we witness here on earth. One particular moment in my life stands out when I describe how the Almighty placed me under his *Shekhinah*. One moment in the life of a college student named Alan Goldsmith hangs in front of me as a blazing reminder of this. And this moment involved a car.

In 1972, I was still in the Midwest in grad school, coaching football, something I loved as much as anything else in my life at that time. So I was happy doing what I loved while I studied for my master's degree. I made so many good friends in college and grad school. We worked and played side by side. The weekdays were for working, coaching, studying, and attending classes. But the weekends—for us as well as so many generations of college boys—were ours for partying.

At that time I was driving a used 1967 Corvette. Not for nothing was this car known as one of Chevy's best and fastest machines. This baby could fly. What a beauty she was, and what a powerhouse of a car. She was blue, shiny, and perfect. I have already mentioned the misadventure with my dad's Chevy when I was in middle school. My next misstep would over-shadow that one into oblivion.

I showed myself to be a levelheaded guy most days, but on this one weekend, I wasn't. Tom Loading and I had really partied hard that night, and of course, we drank…a lot. Tom was my friend and fellow coach at Northwest State Missouri University. We were really drunk, and I should never have been driving, let alone piloting a mighty car like my Corvette.

We decided to go from one party to another in Shenandoah, Iowa, about thirty minutes from Tarkio. Off we went, racing down the road toward that town. I know I was going over ninety miles an hour, and I vaguely remember touching the brake. The next moment that I remember fully was waking up in the grass. I was stretched out on a little grassy hill alongside the highway. My first crazy hysterical thought was of Tom; where was he? What had happened to him? I remember calling his name. Then I started becoming conscious of myself, and I began to feel around to see if I was in one piece, if I could move, if I was bleeding. I noticed my limbs were mov-ing. I saw that I was banged up, but otherwise whole and basically unin-jured. My head hurt; it turned out that I had a slight concussion. I kept calling Tom's name. When we became aware of each other, it was hugely obvious that neither of us had a scratch on us. Not a drop of blood.

The car was another thing altogether. That beautiful Corvette was a pile of fiberglass. One piece on top of another. A rubbish heap of a car, unrecognizable as the gorgeous vehicle we had entered such short minutes ago. I had been so drunk that it had never registered in my alcohol-addled brain that a police car had been chasing us, trying to pull us over.

The police took over immediately at the scene of this devastating accident. Tom and I were transported to the hospital, basically unhurt. I couldn't fathom it then, and I still marvel at the fact that the two of us were really not injured in this crash that ripped my car into small pieces. At that point, I called Tom Devlin to pick us up at the hospital.

Right then, it popped into my consciousness that it was not by chance that I had been unscathed and saved in this horrific accident. This was not mere luck. I knew then what I still know and believe. Tom and I were saved by the Almighty, but not because of my merits. This was not a gift to a righteous young man; instead I knew that I had been saved because of the merits of my parents and grandparents. I had been spared vicious and devastating injuries because of the righteousness of my family. The good deeds they had carried out had saved me, and had also saved me from being responsible for the grievous injury or death of a friend. I knew it with a certainty that has never changed.

I remember thinking about G-d at that moment, and what popped into my mind was a promise to keep the doors to His house open. I wasn't religious then. I had been *bar mitzvahed* at thirteen, and that was that. So, I had no idea what those words meant, "I will keep the doors to Your house open." That statement, that feeling, that belief, has never left my head or heart since that day.

I should have been killed in an accident of such magnitude. I was sure that it was miraculous that we walked away unscathed. I knew that the Almighty had had a path for me. He had a plan, but I had no idea what it was.

I know that I am a person who has a *Derech Hashem*…a path to follow. I knew it the day of my survival after that accident. G-d gave me the physical strength I used to become so strong. He gave me the strength to succeed so grandly in football and to excel in sports. Me, little David, against the Goliath of teams and players so much bigger and stronger. Add to that the honesty and integrity I inherited and learned from my father and grand-parents. Working in the shoe store or, later in my life, being a politician and working with politicians, I have dipped into the well of honesty I was given from my wonderful family for the purpose of playing football, teaching school, selling shoes, or building the Foundation and its good works.

* * *

39

Tom Devlin's Comments

*M*y wife, Carla, and I had rented a house near where I was teaching in Tarkio, Missouri. I was going to grad school at Northwest State Missouri. That brings us to the part of our lives where I mentioned that Goldy went up to Northwest State Missouri, and I helped him get enrolled. Carla and I had rented a house out in the country…really out in the country! We were about eight miles outside of Tarkio in a little old farmhouse situated on a couple hundred acres of land. We had a party one Saturday night. I don't know what the occasion was other than just having a party. We had about fifty or sixty people out at the house. We were having a great time. Goldy came out…he had bought this blue Stingray, and he was with Tom Loading. I think that was the guy's name that he was rooming with at the time. Alan was at my house for a number of hours, and we were imbibing a "bit." I think it was some type of a tropical drink that we liked so much as college kids. One thing you need to know about Goldy is that he doesn't have a huge tolerance for alcohol. In fact another of his nicknames was "Two-can Goldy!"

He and Tom Loading decided they were heading to a bar up in Shenandoah. I think they left our house somewhere around midnight. They left the party and headed out on those dark country roads. You know what you do in a Corvette, you drive fast. That's the only way to drive one of those cars. The roads out there around Tarkio were pretty uninhabited. The highway was good, but evidently Alan was going a little bit too fast around a curve and lost control. Alan wound up flipping the Corvette and being thrown out, and G-d bless, if you ever saw what the car looked like after it stopped rolling! I mean there was absolutely nothing left of it. The only salvageable piece of the car was one wheel. Being fiberglass, it just exploded on impact. There were a million little tiny pieces of fiberglass all over this farmer's field.

I found out about all this in a very alarming way. At about 2:00 that morning, my phone rang. Remember, we were way out in the country. Everybody had gone home, and Carla and I were asleep. I get this sad-sack call from Alan who's at the Fairfax Hospital and needs me to come and get him. So I, of course, got my clothes on and headed right for the hospital. And there they were, Alan and Tom, at 2:30 in the morning sitting on the hospital steps looking kind of bedraggled. Loading, if I remember, just had a scratch on his head. I mean, it was insignificant. The next day we went out and saw the car. That's when we saw the total destruction spread all over a field. I couldn't believe that anybody could possibly have walked away from that wreck. I mean there was nothing left of that car.

As if this story wasn't as unbelievable as science fiction, it gets better. The ironic part of the story was that Goldy had sold the car on Friday, the day before the party and the accident. The guy was supposed to pick it up from Goldy on Monday. That was the kick in the pants. But I don't think Alan minded too much about that after being able to walk away from the accident. What was left was dumped in the back of a pickup truck. That's all that was left…tiny little pieces. The fact that two people walked away from that without serious injuries or death was totally unbelievable.

* * *

40

David Becomes Goliath

When people approached me about writing a book about the work I do through the Jewish Renaissance Family of Organizations, it first seemed like a self-absorbed thing to do. But as I have reflected on the past, the beginnings of my work to bring medical care to poverty-stricken members of my own community, I saw that telling this story went way beyond that. Since the teachings of the Bible mean so much to me, and the telling and retelling of those tales by my grandparents and parents resonates even today through my being, I guess I can look at this book as just another story that I'm telling now.

I've mentioned that I always saw myself as David facing Goliath. Small in stature, set on a football field, against bigger opponents. Small human facing certain death in a violent and possibly fatal car accident. One small person in the back of a shoe store stockpiling medicines and reaching out to local doctors to give their time to our underserved neighbors.

It was just me at the very beginning, but not any more. Now this modern-day David is the head of a growing Foundation full of good people willing to devote their time and efforts to finding the funds, the doctors, the supplies, and the public support for helping the children and adults who are sick, starving, hurt, or hungry, both locally and internationally. David has become Goliath as the Jewish Renaissance Family of Organizations grows and reaches out to more and more sections of society inside and far outside of Middlesex County and New Jersey. As I relate this in July of 2010, we have doctors and medicines on the ground in Haiti. They have been there for weeks, ministering to the injured, starving, and devastated people who survived the catastrophic earthquake that struck in January of this year.

* * *

41

The Arena

A s always, I was looking for ways to give back. I really never ignored that facet of my self; it was and is always present for me. I enjoy searching for and finding ways to share my blessings, my strengths, and my experience with others. I was living in Spotswood, the place where my wife, Annie, and I still live. I was a friend of Joe Spicuzzo, who was a former mayor then. At that time, one of the ways I discovered that allowed me to offer ideas and support to my friends and neighbors, was as councilman. I ran for the position and was elected in 1981. I had some pretty good ideas about the things our community needed and knew that as councilman I would be in a position to carry some of them out. I really wanted to help our town.

Dr. Goldsmith is sworn in as City Council President (at City Hall in Spotswood, NJ) with his wife, Annie, at his side, 1987.

It was in my second term that I began to see into the process more deeply. I have heard politics referred to as a "game," and I believe that term is very apt. Being an effective politician, even after being elected to an office, requires perfecting one's scoring abilities. From football strategies to political strategies...a big jump. It was during this second term when I was council president that an issue rose to prominence in town that I very much wanted to address correctly.

The council wanted to use taxpayers' money to clean up a lake in Spotswood. On the surface that sounded wonderful. However, the lake wasn't entirely the property of our municipality. The lake occupied land that was owned by various people and entities. I seem to remember that ownership was shared by a local church, by the residents living on the lake, and some part by the municipality. Spotswood may have owned about 30 percent of the property. In reality the taxpayers had no reason to foot the entire bill for this, no matter how noble an idea the cleanup was.

That lake was definitely in need of restoration. It had been used as a dump site for years. Junk needed to be removed even before the surrounding area could be cleaned and restored to health. The use of taxpayer money just didn't seem appropriate, in spite of how crucial this renovation appeared. If I remember correctly, the public didn't even have access to the lake, because it was on private property.

I really stood alone on this issue. It was me against the party line. Let me tell you, a lonely place. I just didn't think this was right. But one other councilman supported my position. He and I stood together on this issue. The council couldn't pass the resolution without our votes. I went even farther (don't you just love Democracy?) I sent a letter to the editor of the local paper. In it I voiced my support for our city fathers, who meant well, but were misguided in this intent. I stated my position, saying something like "Would you like taxpayer money to be used to clean up your back yard?" It must have been a very good letter, because I really ticked off everybody. I mean *everybody*. The county chairman wanted my scalp, I think. The council wanted my support for that cleanup issue. I backpedaled, telling everyone I needed more time to think it over. But I knew in my heart that I couldn't vote in favor of that issue and continue to get a good night's sleep. My conscience wouldn't allow me to do it.

I knew that if I wanted any political future, I needed to get onboard. But I couldn't, and I didn't vote in favor of that cleanup. I knew very well that I was signing my own "death-warrant" in local politics. But I'm stubborn, and when I think I'm right, I don't usually yield. The other councilmen knew that the only chance at passing the cleanup bill was by referendum.

So we held that referendum, and the proposal was defeated two to one. Three months later, when the election came up, I ran a good race. But the opposition threw all kinds of money in the mix against my campaign. I lost that election by forty-six votes. In reality, I was relieved. I didn't want to hold another term, but I didn't want anyone to say I gave up without trying.

Even though Spotswood is a relatively small community, it seems that political wheeling and dealing exists there, too. A lot of people in the local government arena had extremely good intentions. I enjoyed working for my town, but, I gained enough of an insight into the functioning of bureaucracy, personal egos, the legislative process, and everything else that goes right along with politics to know it wasn't where I wanted to be. I also grew to know that it was not the arena where I could be most effective at doing what I wanted to do, which was help people.

* * *

42

Goldy Comes Home

By 1973 Perth Amboy's population was evolving. The treelined streets that had resounded with Eastern European languages now echoed with the lilting cadences of Spanish. Newcomers had continued to arrive, and now they hailed from Puerto Rico and many Central and South American nations.

My education in health and phys ed, my bilingualism, my close connections to this town, all served to land me a job in the public school system. I started out teaching at the McGuinness Middle School, a school serving kids from fifth to eighth grade. I was more a health teacher than phys ed teacher. But it worked for me, and I enjoyed my work with these children for three years.

When a position opened in the high school, I took it and went back to coaching and teaching, as well as leading adult education classes at night.

It was a bit of a grind, and I found myself tired out after three years of such a heavy load. I stayed with the daytime coaching and teaching, but stopped working evenings. I loved every minute.

Working with kids in sports is such a wonderful way to guide them. Coaching was my love, and I enjoyed showing the kids how to enjoy football. We also succeeded, which made us all happy. I taught the kids to safely work out and use weights to build strength and self-confidence. It was a privileged position for me. Kids will open up, share thoughts, and bring their problems to a coach or trainer. I had the opportunity to mentor them and offer help when family matters, social problems, school issues, or just being a teenager seemed so troubling for them.

John Masurick, also a Perth Amboy native, was the basketball coach. He was such a good friend, and we worked so well together in the sports department. So there I was, immersed in a job I loved, and doing what I came to realize was my path...helping people who needed help. The kids knew that I was a trusted teacher, one who would listen and help guide them toward solutions. One who wouldn't "squeal" on them, but one who would keep their trust and confidences. I tried to guide them to correct solutions, away from the marijuana that some of them thought would help smooth out their troubles from family crises that threatened their teenage lives. The kids and I developed bonds based on trust and common sense; bonds that have weathered time and still connect many of us today in their adult lives. Actually, I have met many of their children. Of course, I couldn't reach them all, but I felt like this was part of the reason I took this job. I guess that's what I really loved about teaching. I enjoyed helping the kids in academics, but when I could help to keep them on an even keel through those gut-wrenching teenage moments of total disarray, I felt even better about what I was accomplishing.

I brought lots of laughter and lots of love to my role as an educator. When I taught health and phys ed, I integrated so many of the intangible rewards I gathered from my parents and grandparents. There was no yelling when I taught. The kids trusted me. Using what I learned from the personal nuances of my loving family, I reached out to these kids.

The children at the high school reflected the changing immigration patterns into Perth Amboy of the past century; my kids were Hispanic, African American. I gave them a chance, and they gave me one. Maybe it was my ability to speak Spanish. All I know is they came to me with concerns and problems, and I tried to help them. I always kept their wishes foremost; if they wanted privacy, they got it from me. And, if I needed to involve a parent, I did it without betraying the child's confidences. These kids saw my sincerity, and paid me back in kind. I did set boundaries, and the kids respected those. They knew I was the teacher, and they were the students, but they knew they could come to me with trust and openness.

* * *

43

My Father's Failing Health

Toward the end of my teaching tenure, around 1979, I started to feel what many teachers experienced. The bureaucracy weighed heavier and heavier on me. Paperwork took me away from working with the kids directly. I was feeling a need for change. However, the change came to me in a way I never imagined. My father got sick.

I remember that I was finishing my doctorate around 1979 when my dad became too ill to run the shoe store alone. He needed my help. I suppose as in other instances in my life, all I had to do was take a look to see where I was going. I left teaching at that time and moved my attention to working in the shoe business with my father. Of course, now I was the student, and he the teacher.

Dad and Dr. Goldsmith worked together in Goldsmith Shoe Store, 1981.

My father taught me everything I could hope to learn about the shoe business. I learned how to fit shoes properly, deal with customers, handle wholesalers, order shoes, set up displays, and the day-to-day operation of the store. It wasn't easy. Anyone who has never worked in retail has no idea what an all-consuming profession it is. So I went to work with my dad in the shoe store every day, and also found a way to complete my degree.

* * *

44

Finding My Sole

I needed to finish my doctoral dissertation. I had already completed my course work and dissertation credits, but I had no time to continue with the doctoral program at Rutgers. I transferred my credits to another university and completed my degree long distance. My dissertation will never be considered one of the great achievements of academia, but it was pretty good. I was really up to my neck in shoes by that time. So both parts of my life transpired together, and I received my PhD. I became a shoe clerk with a PhD, and sold shoes with my dad for the next three years.

We had no idea as to the seriousness or magnitude of my dad's problems. He had always worked hard, and like most families, we assumed he would just keep on moving forward and onward. As it turned out, his health took a dramatic and sudden rush downward. It didn't happen while he was working, but while he was relaxed and having fun.

My father loved going to Atlantic City to gamble a bit. He and Mom were not high rollers; they just enjoyed the exciting atmosphere and feeling of being on a small vacation. The new Atlantic City of casinos and shows had just evolved, and my mom and dad took full advantage of the proximity of that reborn beach town. They started traveling to that gambling mecca almost every Monday. He, and sometimes my mother, would take the bus and make a day trip. He'd spend all day at the slots or playing blackjack, then bus home in the evening. The last time he went, though, he suffered a massive heart attack. I don't think anyone there that day realized how sick he was. The overt symptoms of an acute heart attack sometimes mimic other illnesses. So someone helped him pull himself together, get himself cleaned up, and get on a bus back home.

How could we have known how sick my father was? My dad, the provider for our little family, had never been sick a day in his life. We never saw him any other way but in charge and forging ahead. Of course, he was immediately hospitalized. I was working in his store and visiting him after closing. I saw him every night. We were all in a state of disbelief. I couldn't make myself face the looming truth. Dad was in the hospital for three days and actually started looking a bit better. My mother seemed to know or accept that he wasn't getting better. She told me as much, but I held onto hope that he would be back in the store soon. Dad asked me to look after my mom. I can still hear myself telling him not to talk like that; he'd be back home soon. I really felt that he was going to pull out of this. I never thought, couldn't let it into my thoughts, that something irreversible and final would happen to him now.

That night I received a frantic call from my mother. She urged me to get to the hospital as fast as I could. She really sounded horrible. I think he had already passed away, and she couldn't tell me over the phone. It was Mother's Day, 1983. I remember very little of the frantic trip Annie and I made to the hospital. I do know I was in no condition to drive. But I was sure I was going to speak to him again. I never even thought once that he was gone. I was going to see my dad. But I was wrong. I can't remember ever crying before that day. I simply "lost it." Mom, Dena, Annie, and I said our goodbyes right there in that small hospital room. How hard this was for me. My father, gone. Unimaginable.

* * *

45

Ann Goldsmith's Comments

*A*lan had been helping his father in the State Street shoe store. That wasn't the basis of their deep relationship, only the part that showed. He was, had always been, very close to his father. They had a huge and deep relationship, and toward the end they worked side by side. Louis's death was very sudden and unexpected. He was too young to go. I lost Alan for a whole year then. He just shut down. It was almost like he was unreachable. It was as if he withdrew from life. It was very hard getting him back into the world of the living. He functioned; he went through the motions of functioning every day. Alan was then, and still is, very private about his feelings, his emotions. This was a terrible time for him.

* * *

46

Finding My Soul

There I was, thirty-six years old, suffering the loss of my dear father. We all share a planet, the same oxygen, the same food and entertainment. We really share the same themes in our lives no matter how separated we are by geography, religion, or culture. Birth, life, death. We mourn with friends when they lose a parent. I even knew loss, having experienced the loss of my very beloved grandparents. Yet nothing, absolutely nothing, had prepared me for the blow I suffered at losing my dad at the young age of sixty-eight. I thought I knew about grief, but no, I didn't.

After suffering a terrible loss, familiar routines often serve as an escape from the pain. But returning to work, for me, only opened the wound of grief even more.

I had to eventually go back to the store, and that only reminded me of him every second of every day. The store that was his, that was always part of his identity, and now mine. It was filled with constant reminders of my father. Dad always kept an extra pair of shoes for himself in the back room. I couldn't even look at that pair of shoes without losing my composure. Finally, I had to hide them in a box. Tears were always near the surface. I had to return to the daily rituals my father and I had shared, so there didn't seem to be any escape for me. Following the path we had walked together was becoming impossible. I didn't want to go to trade shows in New York, because we used to do that together. I could hardly consider walking back into the store. I was a wreck. I knew time was a healer, but I couldn't figure out how to survive long enough to let time do its job. Closure and solace were hard to come by. That's when I turned to my faith. Judaism became my refuge and my answer. My religion offered me a place to grieve, to cry, to suffer, but it also offered me a place of peace, solace, and healing. Everyone loses a parent. Everyone moves from being a son or daughter to being the head of the family. It is a natural progression of life. So, why was I having so much trouble moving on? Why was I looking into the future and not seeing peace? The synagogue offered me help to begin to change my inconsolable grief into acceptance and beyond.

Our synagogue was undergoing changes at that time. We had a new rabbi; I didn't know him at all. But he became instrumental in my growth. He helped me move from the deep unrelenting grief weighing me down, to a different place. And his guidance led me ultimately into the type of Jewish life I had never had or imagined before. Rabbi Chomsky became a strong ally for me in my grief. He and his son came to our home every day during the grieving period. He presence was a great comfort to me.

I needed more than the ritual seven days of grieving. This loss of my dear father was not going to be one that I could push into the back of my mind easily. I began to attend synagogue every morning to say *kaddish*, the prayer for the dead. This was me, Alan, the guy who showed up at temple only on the high holidays. So once, maybe twice, a year it had been my custom to sit in temple and pray. Now I was there every day. The ritual became a solace for me, and Rabbi Chomsky my partner in this process, this journey from that devastating moment into the rest of my life.

I said *kaddish* every day for my father. I wrapped my forearm and fore-head in the traditional prayer boxes, called *tefillin*. My march into my Jewish self took its first steps. The progression took me that entire year. We never forget who our parents were and how much they meant to us, how much we love them…but we need to go on. It was a very hard thing for me to do.

* * *

47
Finding My Way

Although I sat *shiva* (the Jewish traditional seven-day mourning period), for me it wasn't enough. I couldn't get over my dad's death in just a week. So, every morning for a year, I went to synagogue and intoned the *kaddish*. I needed to find my own peace, and I wanted to honor my wonderful father, so I mourned over and over, every day. When my year of mourning ended, it became obvious to me that the *shul* (synagogue) needed something from me. The previous president of the synagogue wanted me to take over that position. He wanted me to present myself for that post.

The *shul* needed some new ideas, new guidance, and new thoughts, and the past leader thought I should offer that help. Here was something I could do to give back—a recurring theme in my upbringing and my life. I knew my grandparents would have wholeheartedly approved of this idea.

This *shul*, Shaarey Tefiloh, was the one my Goldsmith grandparents had attended and where they had worshipped. The more I thought about this idea and this new project, the more I liked it. I accepted. I could actually feel my grandparents smiling down on me.

There's a joke that circulated in Israel about President Reagan talking to President Rabin. This is going back a bit, but it's still relevant. Rabin was speaking to Reagan about being president. He commented to our president that, "In the United States, you only have one president. But in Israel everybody's president!" So I really found out what that joke meant during my tenure as leader of a synagogue.

Times continued to change in Perth Amboy. People were on the move as the suburbs grew. One of the results of this social upheaval was that the size of our congregation continued dropping. In fact it was dwindling to an unsustainably small number of families and worshippers.

* * *

48

The $18 Yeshiva

Eight years after my father's passing, I was still selling shoes. It was 1991, and Goldsmith Shoe Store was still my business; that's where I spent my days. I opened and ran the store every day just as my grandfather and father had done. That's where I met Rabbi Gruskin. The rabbi entered my shoe store one day. He and I struck up a rather friendly and lively conversation. He was making the rounds of neighboring establishments seeking donations for a *yeshiva* (a school) in Livingston, New Jersey. Good conversation is a powerful force. We began a wonderful friendship that transcended that day in my store when I gave him a donation for the *yeshiva*. I donated *chai* to his school. In Hebrew, *chai* means "life," but the word also holds a numeric value, as all Hebrew words do. *Chai* is eighteen, so I donated eighteen dollars to his *yeshiva*.

We continued our friendship and the animated discussions about Judaism right there in my shoe store. Many a day you could see us seated together, he the teacher and mentor, I the student. One day, I mentioned to him that it would be wonderful to open a *yeshiva* here in Perth Amboy. I told him that we had some space on the bottom floor of our synagogue. He could use that space as a *Beit Midrash* (a house of learning) for instructing children. Rabbi Gruskin liked the idea. We started the ball rolling right there in the store.

Rabbi Gruskin contacted Rabbi Reich, one of the outstanding *Rosh Yeshivas* (leader of a Talmudical academy). His brother-in-law, Rabbi Cutler, was the head of the Lakewood *Yeshiva*. Both of them came to Perth Amboy and were instrumental in opening that *yeshiva*. Even as we saw the numbers of the Jewish population falling off, we started a renewal. Perth Amboy housed a new school. Teaching the children was, and is, the way to perpetuate the faith…the way to carry forward the teachings, not only of our own fathers, but our forefathers. What a wonderful moment that was.

I still had the mentality of "the teacher" left inside me from the wonderful years of coaching and teaching here in Perth Amboy. So here I was, helping and mentoring again. Only this time I was learning, too. For the next nine years the young men and the rabbis were my mentors and teachers. Our *yeshiva* started out with fifteen young men and grew to include about forty over the years. Here again was the proof for me, laid out right in front of my eyes, of my long-standing belief that G-d had a plan for me, and His hand was guiding me always.

Since my college years, specifically my survival of the terrible car accident I caused and suffered in my blue Corvette, I have felt that I have been walking in the direction in which G-d has been pointing me. And here was another step on that path. I had promised the Almighty that I would keep His doors open. And now I was president of a synagogue. I was one of the people instrumental in establishing and opening the doors of a *yeshiva*. I was continuing to fulfill my promise.

The young men who studied in that *yeshiva* have had a huge effect on my life; as big an effect as I have had on theirs. In fact, I have attended countless weddings. There is a group of these men with whom I'm still in regular contact. I speak to one of them on a weekly basis, even today. We speak and discuss Torah. Another blessing.

My wife, Annie, and I don't have children of our own. For whatever reason, we have not given rise to more Goldsmiths. But in spite of that, we live a life filled with nurturing and teaching. As the sages say, when a person supports and teaches Torah to children, it is as if he has given birth to those children.

Our lives are intertwined with those of so many of the wonderful young people who have passed through the school. The *yeshiva* extended our reach to more than one generation of young men. Having said that, I must say they have given back in equal measure. Our lives and our hearts are brimming over with the warmth of these young men. These kids have really had an everlasting and powerful effect on my life.

After *Yom Kippur* one year, some of the young men were discussing *Sukkot*, an upcoming holiday celebrating and remembering our ancestors' travels through the desert before they entered the Holy Land. During those forty years, they were protected by "clouds of glory" that hung over and around them, protecting them from nature's discomforts. We celebrate and remember G-d's protection and goodness by building a temporary home, called a *sukkah*. One of the boys asked us if we had a *sukkah*.

The *sukkah* is the temporary "house," a wooden structure that is built for this holiday. Its roof remains open to the sky. The family traditionally resides in it and takes meals here during this holiday. When Annie and I replied that we didn't have one, the young men responded with a call to action. They built us a *sukkah*.

The boys secretly came to our house, bringing all the construction materials. They spent their own money on the materials and spent time constructing it in our backyard. These boys were students in every way; they didn't earn a living and subsisted on a student budget. So their money was very tight. Yet they pooled resources and built this for us. They wouldn't take any money from me for their expenditures or their time. Annie and I were thrilled and very moved to receive this gift.

Our first *sukkah* had been generated from the heart of giving and sharing. How close these boys reached to the center of my heart with a generosity and philosophy of giving that mirrored the spirit, the spark, I had inherited from my grandparents and parents.

I will continue to work toward the establishment and maintenance of *yeshivas* here in our community and others. It's part of my life, this continuing input into the lives of young people, their formation, their lives, and their religious paths. To me giving back seems as natural as breathing.

Rabbi Gruskin, the rabbi who served as the catalyst to my ongoing support of these schools, also became my teacher. In fact, not only did we often sit together in study right there in my shoe store, he and I continue to share a close friendship and relationship today. He is still my teacher.

Rabbi Gruskin and I, since the day I gave him eighteen dollars for that *yeshiva*, have shared stories and adventures galore. We have complemented each other from the very beginning in my little shoe store on State Street. In fact, I laughingly told Rabbi Gruskin one day, "You take care of souls, and I take care of soles." Looks like I've started taking care of souls, too. Grandpa Hymie would be pleased.

* * *

49

What Is A Home?

I love Perth Amboy. One of the reasons I feel this way about my hometown is because when I was a kid growing up here, everybody knew everybody else. This town was comfortable and safe and filled with people who knew me and my family. Back then families weren't as mobile as they are today. Many people didn't even own cars. New Jersey was the focal point of our lives, and Perth Amboy the nexus. We gathered here. Our "cousin's club" met at my grandparents' home. Boisterous loving group that we were, we ate and laughed and played together. I don't know which I remember more, the abundant food or the loud card games. I only know that I took some strong lessons from those family get-togethers… the need to have a home base, the importance of family, and the mission to take care of one another. I miss that type of closeness today. We don't have that type of geographical unity any more. Our family is scattered all over the United States.

But for me, Perth Amboy is the center of the universe. I established the Jewish Renaissance Foundation in the back room of the well-established Goldsmith Shoe Store, on State Street, moved our offices to the historical Proprietary House (the Royal Governor's Mansion in the late 1700s) when we finally developed a good head of steam, and finally saw the culmination of years of hard work in the inauguration of the Jewish Renaissance Medical Center on Hobart Street. Perth Amboy, then, is not just a place, a city, a dot on a map. Perth Amboy is my home, my memories. Perth Amboy is my heart.

* * *

50

The Vision

People are always asking me questions about the Jewish Renaissance Family of Organizations. They want to know how I started something like this. Where did the idea come from? How did I begin? Where did the inspiration emanate from? How did it grow so huge?

There's no easy answer. As is true in life, everything has a short and a long answer. However, this is a big one. In short, I have ideas. That's the simple answer. I see a need, and I attempt to fill it. Someone else's problem may be within my power to aid or even alleviate. I'm not a random do-gooder, or maybe I am. I have very strong beliefs in the Almighty and I do believe that the impetus to create the Foundation, Medical Center, and Boys & Girls Club, plus the charitable and social network under its growing umbrella, ultimately come from His power.

* * *

51

Ann Goldsmith's Comments

*A*lan always expressed the idea that while he was growing up, he wanted to be a rabbi. He felt that he had a direct line "upstairs." Does Alan truly believe that what he has created today, his success today, is from a higher power? It's a given.

* * *

52

Family Power

You know, I can't remember ever hearing my parents argue. My memories are filled with goodness, love, and peaceful moments. My parents and grandparents were always in and out of each other's houses. We lived so close to one another, and our doors were never locked. So the arrival of a Goldsmith or a Paley grandparent in our home was a regular occurrence. There was always a *pushke* (a collection box) in my grandparents' home, where we were encouraged to drop pennies, nickels, or any small coin. It was not the amount that mattered, it was the action. Shabbat was that evening when I remember always being with them, my wonderful grandparents, and being encouraged to drop a coin in the *pushke*. Giving to others, giving back, lending a hand…these were the bywords guiding my life at the knees of my parents and grandparents. I guess when it starts early it just never stops.

* * *

53
Visionary

Some people who know me call me a visionary. I don't know, I guess I am the leader. I'm the one who sees where we can go and sees possibilities where other people see only problems. I know it seems like a fantasy, but thoughts like that take me back to my roots, always to my roots. That means to my family, my people, my Jewish roots.

I'm a Levite, one of the twelve tribes. I come from the same tribe as Moses, so this type of thinking always brings me back to his story. I think of Moses leading the Jewish people through the desert for so many years, and I see a lesson for me. His long journey, and the tests he faced in his role as leader, give all of us guidance. I hope I have learned something from that story and have absorbed some knowledge about leadership. And I say this with a smile and with great humility.

I enjoy reading and discussing Bible stories. I enjoy Torah study. Those stories relate so directly to our lives. Modern as we are, the themes, passions, dilemmas, joys, and celebrations from long ago, those reflections of the lives of our forefathers, are relevant today. I don't believe that what I am saying is endemic to Judaism, though. I think all of us…Jews, Catholics, Muslims, Protestants, as well as all other believers and religions, strive to follow in the good works and the teachings of our forefathers. The tales and lessons are so important, form such a strong life foundation, and entertain us at the same time.

In a roundabout way, I can relate the story of the Tower of Babel, for example, to the mission of the Jewish Renaissance Family of Organizations. This is not a biblical interpretation, but my loose take on this great story. The peoples of the earth, coming from different nations, all spoke one language. They wanted to build a gigantic tower to reach up to the sky to demonstrate how united and strong they were. We marvel today at the latest tallest skyscraper, so I can imagine the impact of such a project in ancient times. All the nations of the earth united to create this display of their knowledge and strength. G-d saw them working to build this huge tower, and saw it was wrong for men to try to reach the heavens.

G-d acted, not by killing the people but by stopping them. G-d scattered the people over the face of the earth and gave them different languages, so they couldn't communicate and collaborate on this project. They couldn't understand each other, and they drifted apart. They went their own ways, developed different cultures, different features. Why did this happen? Why are we so different, and yet all needing the very same things to survive and thrive? I believe that G-d wanted us to see our similarities and differences, and learn to revel in each others differences. I think G-d wanted us to have to work and to strive for peace, and wanted us to search for the commonalities that could ultimately bring us together in understanding of our humanness, of our similarities, of our love for life. I believe that G-d wanted us to enjoy our differences and to see through the various languages, customs, and religions to make us want to help each other.

G-d doesn't make mistakes; G-d wants us to re-read the stories of humankind and learn. What did G-d want? I believe G-d wanted to give us reasons to bring us back together. One world working for the betterment of humankind. One people, one heart.

* * *

54

Yvonne Lopez's Comments (2010)

*A*lan is a visionary. He has great dreams. He has the vision. When Alan sees a need and that there's room to fill that gap, nothing stops him. Nothing stops Alan. He has such a massive wonderful leadership team. He can have a dream and a vision and come back to his leadership team and say, "This is what I envision. Help me get there. Help us get there." That's how he operates.

When I think about Alan, and I think about how he carries himself...the diplomacy...he has very good people skills. When you see Alan upset, maybe he's bursting, maybe red in the face. He would never show it in his actions. That's not who he is. He's very diplomatic. He's a peacemaker. I've seen Alan over the last fourteen years. We've all matured as we've aged. We've become wise. You can have a healthy debate with Alan. And if it's not healthy, he's the first to own up to it.

* * *

55

Drowning

Look back over your entire life. Try to trace a path, or a straight line, or a continuum from childhood to where you stand at this very moment. Don't you find that you couldn't continue to trek that line, that you must swerve and veer into other paths? You'll find little driveways and parking lots that line the path of your life, where you stopped for a while and experienced some moments that (often with the clarity that comes by looking back) defined you, guided you farther, or brought you toward your destiny and life's work?

It's that way for me. There are little places where I *had* to travel on this journey, that I now know were key to my becoming who I am today. These moments were helpful in my original determination to start and build the Jewish Renaissance Foundation. These defining moments continue to motivate what has grown into today's Jewish Renaissance Family of Organizations, allowing us to offer care, medicine, shelter, and guidance to children and adults in need.

One of those smaller pathways always leads me to the beach in Perth Amboy. If you grew up in New Jersey, with our long and beautiful shoreline, you probably spent time at "the shore." The term helps to define us. During my high school years, I worked as a lifeguard at the Perth Amboy Shore.

Of course my job was to watch over the swimmers, and I did. But an incident occurred the summer before my senior year. I remember one young girl, maybe four or five years old, whose head went under the water. She wasn't in deep water, but it was deep enough that she was submerged and needed help. I raced into the water and pulled her out. The feeling of having saved someone's life was overwhelming, especially for the young teenager I was then. The moment stayed with me into my adulthood. But on two other occasions, when I tried to save someone, the endings were different. One episode happened when I was in college.

As young men we often feel "all powerful" in our own minds and see the world as a ribbon of possibilities at our feet. I was in graduate school, and I was coaching football. During a practice session, someone came running down to the field in a panic. She was screaming about a girl who lay unconscious in her room. She had had an epileptic attack and hit her head on the radiator as she fell. When we arrived at her side, she had already turned blue. Coach Lade and I bent down and worked to revive her. We worked until the ambulance came, but she was gone. It was a dreadful moment for all of us. Trying, and failing to help her, made it especially painful.

I experienced another life-and-death moment that shaped my life. My wife, Annie, and I were on vacation in St. Thomas. I was scuba diving, quite unaware of the drama unfolding on the surface. As I came up, I heard a cry. A man from a cruise ship was floating on the surface as if he was snorkeling, but he was unconscious. I joined another fellow in pulling him to the beach. He had suffered a heart attack, but we didn't know that. I realized he had no pulse, so we immediately began administering CPR. In this tiny beach resort, the ambulance couldn't make its way all the distance to the beach as quickly as we all hoped it would. We just kept up his pulse until it arrived.

I later heard that he didn't make it. I have always felt that these moments, when the small dividing line between life and death showed itself in such an obvious fashion, made a huge impact on me. My father always said that we need to make the best use of the short time we have on this earth. He said that the title in front of a name, like Dr., President, Ambassador, or Indian Chief, wasn't important. He stressed that it is what's in back of your name that is important: honest, trustworthy, compassionate, helpful, loving, caring. When we leave this earth, all we leave behind is what's behind our name. In these instances I had a firsthand look at the brevity of life, resulting in my certainty of the importance of leaving behind a legacy of good works.

* * *

56

Dena Needed Help

While writing this book, I spent quite a bit of time looking inside myself, searching for answers to the queries people have been asking me for years. Why did you begin amassing medical supplies in the back room of your shoe store? What plans did you have? Were you going to sell shoes forever, or close up shop? Where did the kernel of the idea you named the "Jewish Renaissance Foundation" start? Here's another part of the answer.

I haven't spoken much about my sister, Dena. She and I grew up in a close relationship. We always enjoyed a strong brother-sister bond that hasn't weakened. She is a few years younger than I am, but I always teased her that she acted like the older sibling. We have always shared loving ties, so if we ever needed one another, we both knew help was right there.

It's a very good thing that we can't see into the future. I think the challenges we would see would scare us so much that we would never be able to handle them when they finally came. There was a huge challenge coming, and it involved my sister.

Around 1995 when Dena was in her mid-forties, she suddenly found herself going blind in one eye. The condition occurred without warning. At the time this started, my family didn't contact me. No one told me what was happening to my sister. I guess my mother and Dena felt they could handle things, but that proved not to be the case. My sister saw an ophthalmologist, but it seemed that there was nothing he could do. This doctor recommended and highly stressed that Dena see a neurologist…at once. That was one of those heart-stopping moments; he might as well have told her to take a ride to the moon. Dena was a single mom raising two children on her own. She also had no health care benefits. My mother finally got me involved. Who knows what goes through a mother's mind when she attempts to help a daughter in need, but she finally called me.

Here's where my tight community of wonderful friends and teachers from Perth Amboy, the *yeshiva*, and school entered into play. Rabbi Gruskin's longtime friend, Dr. Younger, was a neurologist in North Jersey. I contacted him about Dena and told him her story. He immediately said, "Don't worry. Send her to me. I won't charge you at all." But whatever it would have cost, I would have paid.

We took Dena to see him. She needed an MRI of her brain. We were at full tilt now. I called another friend, Ruben Taber, the owner of an MRI center in Baltimore, who had grown up with us in Perth Amboy. He had the type of practice that provided the tests Dena needed. His response was as true and heartfelt as my other friend's. "Come on down, Goldy. We'll take care of your sister."

Dena had the MRI. Dr. Younger originally thought that Dena might have to see a neurosurgeon. We knew something big was occurring. Once again, my network of friends came through. I found more help at our *Yeshiva*. Rabbi Gruskin also had a cousin, a neurosurgeon in Detroit, who could perform the operation on Dena, if it became necessary. We were frantic, but my friends responded.

The Detroit doctor offered the same openhearted charity as my other friends. He said, "I'll take care of your sister. I won't charge you." He needed to work out some business details with the hospital, because Dena was from out of state. Dr. Younger contacted us once again and gave us more news. As is often the case with medical news, some was good and some was bad. Sometimes it's hard to distinguish, when your heart is involved.

Miracles do happen, and Dena's blindness turned out to be temporary. But we were a long way from finished. Dr. Younger wanted to see my sister again. He said that Dena's MRI did not show a brain tumor, which sounded wonderful. On the other hand, he notified us that she might actually have latent multiple sclerosis. He did think that this condition, and the blindness (should it recur), could be controlled by medication. But the story had a fairly good ending. Dena received the help she needed and is doing well. The condition has never recurred.

The way I saw it, the message was growing clearer and clearer. If this could happen to us, a family with strong ties to the community, with a history of working and living in one closely-knit town, with a history of working hard and earning a living, what was going on out there with regard to health care for people with fewer connections and no lifelines? Who was taking care of them and their children? What were they doing when they needed to see a doctor? How were they arranging to pay for x-rays, blood tests, prescriptions?

I saw good-hearted doctors willing to lend a charitable hand. Surely, I thought, there must be more doctors who would pitch in once in a while. There must be other ways to keep such a powerful lifeline open. Again, the pathway presented itself to me. The same pathway I had been following seemed to open up in a new direction right in front of my eyes. In my heart I believe and felt G-d's presence again sending me the signposts to follow.

* * *

57

The Difficult
Search For Funds

*I*n 1996 at the Jewish Renaissance Foundation's inception, we took the first steps in developing Operation Lifeline U.S.A. The original goal of Operation Lifeline was to bring medical care and services to local people in need. But first, I needed to become more aggressive in securing funds. I actively started looking for money to support these ideas. This was not an easy thing to do. Remember, we were nobodies, working at the rear of a shoe store.

We started tapping sources in banks. We reached out to these institutions, but they were not quick to offer money to "nobodies." We found doctors who would donate some time, we found a venue, and held health fairs. All through Middlesex County, doctors began to volunteer their services, and people in need started attending these fairs. Our health fairs offered options for pediatric care, internal medicine, diabetes, cholesterol screening and vaccinations. One of our first health fairs attracted seven hundred fifty people on one Sunday afternoon. Operation Lifeline U.S.A. began to take shape. That was around the time when Governor Christine Whitman became involved.

Governor Whitman's chief of staff came to Perth Amboy. The reports she brought back to the governor obviously created a good impression. The governor loved what we were doing. Governor Whitman gave Operation Lifeline U.S.A. forty thousand dollars from the Governor's Discretionary Fund for our first year. Word started to get around. We were making a name for our Foundation and its work.

We contacted United Way and put in an application to this organization. They saw fit to pick us up as part of their operations, and we received some funding from them for one year. I think they gave us about fifty thousand dollars. We did anything we could for funds. For example, Dr. Aaron Feingold, one of the members of our board of directors, wrote a book. He gave us one hundred copies, which we sent out in our search for donations. Donation by donation, grant by grant, we were under way.

I also added a substantial amount of my own money. Every year since that time, we have grown. We had to be overly careful with expenses, so growth was very slow. I hired someone part-time, at first, to serve as a secretary and, eventually, I was able to add two more people.

The problems we faced were huge. When I think back to what we were attempting, I have to laugh. We were a tiny start-up. Maybe it was the hubris of youth or the blind faith we had in what we were doing that kept us plunging forward, in spite of the ongoing problems and setbacks. Difficulties with the irregularity of salary disbursements, due to the uncertainty of securing grant monies, was a nagging problem. I lost some good people because of that financial glitch. Yet, a core group of people toughed it out, stood by me and the Foundation, and we made it through the tough times.

I started applying for grants from corporations, trust funds, and charitable foundations. Usually, a foundation like ours, in the shaky and preliminary beginning stage we were in, had pretty slim chances of succeeding.

Most nonprofits last somewhere from one to seven years. Here I was, in 1996, running a charitable organization from the back of a shoe store. Shoes were piled up all over that back room, and that's where the initial steps were taken for the charitable works that bloomed and blossomed into the Jewish Renaissance Family of Organizations. As of 2010, we have been in the helping business for fourteen years.

"Split-personality" describes the life I was living then. I was selling shoes all day, measuring feet, giving advice on styles and colors—living the same life my grandfather and father had lived. I was continuing the Goldsmith legacy of giving good service to people who needed comfortable shoes. But, just as I saw my grandfathers and father do, I was giving back. I was living out the lessons they had taught me about passing the spark in my heart on to other people.

The good works were emanating from the back of the Goldsmith Shoe Store, where I incorporated the Jewish Renaissance Foundation in 1996. By 1997, already working the Foundation from a small office, I closed the shoe store for good. What an emotional benchmark that was. We moved from the back of the shoe store to a small office in the Proprietary House at 149 Kearny Avenue. Some of our offices are still in this lovely history-filled eighteenth-century building.

* * *

58

Operation Lifeline U.S.A.—And Shoes, Of Course

*A*fter experiencing my sister's nightmare, and our scramble to find help for her, I realized more and more that we weren't the only ones who would need help in the face of a health crisis. I was invigorated with a fantastic vision that started to take shape in the back room of the Goldsmith Shoe Store. My plan involved recruiting doctors and dentists. I envisioned giving them a small goal and involving enough of them to make a difference. My original idea was that if each of them saw five patients a year—just five—we could start to offer health care to people in need. This was my initial premise. At its inception, this was the idea for Operation Lifeline U.S.A., the first program undertaken by the Jewish Renaissance Foundation.

Taking a step that had not been attempted before, I organized health fairs, where people could actually see a doctor. I recruited generous doctors who agreed to accept five charity care patients a year. Because of these doctors' openhearted humanitarian actions, these people now had the possibility of becoming known to a doctor...their own doctor. This traditionally underserved group was now going to be able to receive ongoing medical care, not just emergency care. This meant that these charity care patients could now see their own doctor regularly during the year.

We were off to a good start, but had a long way to go in providing complete care. If a doctor's charity care patient needed surgery, for example, that person still had no access. For each case, we had to scramble to find a doctor who would perform the surgery at no cost. We also had to locate a hospital that would accept the patient for charity care. This was time-consuming, frustrating, and often led us to a dead end.

But, step one was already in place; we were sending people to the doctor. It was one small step with many ramifications. The doctor needed a point person working on the phone, so when we called the office the doctor's staff would know that this particular patient came from the Jewish Renaissance Foundation. In other words, they had to know not to charge this patient. This way, we could help maintain and preserve the patient's dignity, because he or she would arrive at that office like any other patient. We started small, and it was hectic.

At that time, I was doing all the legwork with one other person from my staff, from the back room of the shoe store. We were looking for doctors all the time. We encountered overwhelming difficulties. I started out with two people on "staff." We received small grants from the state, but those funds never arrived on time. I had payroll problems. I wouldn't take any salary if my employees didn't receive their money, and this occurred frequently. There were times I didn't take a penny and could only give them half pay until the money arrived. I lost one great employee after another because they couldn't live on money "once in a while." I hired Judy

Goldberg, whose primary function was to raise money. After years of service, she was promoted to CEO. She did a great job putting things in order. She retired just last year after devoting herself to the Jewish Renaissance Foundation for nine years.

* * *

59

Perth Amboy Evolves

*A*t the same time we were taking the beginning small steps into the Foundation's work, I was active in our *shul*. Perth Amboy was continuing to change, and those changes were altering the cultural makeup of our town.

By accepting the presidency of our synagogue, I was in a position to see, firsthand, the effects of change on the Jewish population of our town. Jewish families were disappearing. Natural attrition had reduced my parents' generation, but social trends were affecting their children and grandchildren. The younger people and their growing families were moving to the suburbs. The reasons were many and varied, but the result was that our congregation was in danger of disappearing.

We began to actively recruit families to replace the growing loss of members. Jewish families began moving in from other sections of the East

Coast. Many of them arrived in need. They brought their families to start a new life in Perth Amboy and needed jobs, housing, and health care. I saw that I could do a lot more for the Perth Amboy community outside of the synagogue. Added to that was a growing influx of new immigrants from different countries, many of whom needed help, too. That was another impetus for recruiting doctors for Operation Lifeline U.S.A. and for our health fairs. This was a way I could give more back to the community. This was the first initiative that I began that formed the start of the Foundation.

The synagogue gave the burgeoning Foundation fifteen hundred dollars to get this program going. I put in monies of my own. Our goal was to reach out to everyone who needed our help, anyone who needed health care. Religion was not an issue; this was not a Jewish organization for Jewish people. This was to be a Jewish organization for all people of all religions. Our motto was, and continues to be, "One People, One Heart." I could see Grandpa Hymie with that nickel in his hand, smiling.

* * *

60

The Phone
In The Back Room

My business only had one phone line. We were such small potatoes that there wasn't even money for an extra line or another phone. We used a system with two different rings to separate store business from Foundation matters. One ring signaled that the incoming phone call was for the store. Two rings meant a call for the Foundation.

Another institution involved with Goldsmith Shoe Store was the lunch group. This was a group of friends who had been meeting at the store every afternoon for a very long time. When I picture us in my distant memory, I see a scene reminiscent of an old-time Western movie with the bunch of ornery wisecracking locals sitting around the pot-bellied stove. Only with us, it wasn't just talk. There was laughter. Lots of it. They were as much a part of that store as I was. So the gang was there on this particular day when the phone rang twice. One of the "lunch gang" picked up the phone, and said, "Goldsmith Shoe Store." A man, surprised by that greeting, apologized for getting the wrong number, and hung up. By the time I realized the error, the call was lost. I reminded the guy who had picked up the phone about the ringtone system. I chided him about losing a call for the Foundation.

The phone rang again, two rings signaling a Foundation call. This time I zipped past him and grabbed the phone. A voice with a heavy Hungarian accent asked for Dr. Goldsmith. When I said, "That's me," he said, "I could swear I dialed the same number a minute ago and got a shoe store!" Laughing, I told him, "Yeah, that always happens."

When I picture this whole scene, where we came from, where we are, and where we're headed, it still makes me laugh. That tiny storage room could have served as a backdrop for the Marx Brothers.

Medical supplies towered in shoulder-high piles next to the season's latest shoe styles. A hodgepodge of boxes, chairs, a desk...not your typical setup for the office of a charitable organization. Even the process for using our fax machine seemed as if written for a comedic movie scene. If you heard the two-ring signal for the Foundation, you could pick up the phone in the front of the store. But then, if you heard a strange whooshing sound alerting you to an incoming fax transmission, you'd have to run to the back of the store to turn on the fax machine. Groucho, Harpo, and Chico would have been totally at home running around our place in those early years. But in fifteen years, things have changed, and now we travel all over the globe under the auspices of the United Nations.

* * *

61

Ambassador Calling

*T*he man with the accent, who had called the day of the ringtone mix-up, just happened to be the ambassador to Hungary for the United Nations. We were in the beginning steps of a collaboration with the ambassador to take a medical mission to his country. The scope of Operation Lifeline U.S.A. had broadened. We were about to have an international presence. Operation Lifeline International was born. He asked for our help to rejuvenate one of the old rundown hospitals from the time of the Second World War.

This hospital was a wreck. It was actually a remnant of a hospital that was opened for survivors of the Holocaust. The need there was tremendous. In addition to its rundown state, the facility was long outdated and in need of basic medicines and supplies. They could barely meet the needs of their slightly ill patients, let alone very sick people needing specialized care. We helped them get started on revamping that facility, but haven't had the opportunity to go back.

There's lots more to tell about how my little nonprofit grew from the back of the shoe store to the opening in October of 2008 of the fifteen million dollar state-of-the-art Jewish Renaissance Medical Center right here in Perth Amboy.

Dr. Goldsmith in Zhitomir, Ukraine at the Children's Clinic where the Jewish Renaissance Foundation supplied pharmaceuticals and three pediatric doctors to serve the children through "Operation Lifeline", 1999.

* * *

62

Ray Geneski's Comments

I *retired in 1994. A group of us used to meet in Alan's store every day around 12:00, maybe 1:00 for coffee. We'd sit there and talk and just have a good time. A lot of joking and laughing was flying in there, let me tell you. Alan was running the shoe store, but he had other ideas. Alan had already started getting interested in forming this charity. He worked on it from the store, built it up, eventually sold the store, and went into running the Jewish Renaissance Foundation full time.*

Alan was there for a number of years, running the shoe business. Then he got this idea, a calling I guess you'd call it. We kidded him a lot.

I mean, there we were, this bunch of guys sitting around joshing every day in the store. There's always been a "no holds barred policy" on ribbing and joking among this group.

Pretty soon we'd be selling shoes while he was out running around doing Jewish Renaissance Foundation business. We tried to help him out in that way. We were there. If he wanted to take off an hour or so, he could.

We laughed a lot. I can remember so many funny stories. It got a little out of hand; some things you can't really put on paper. We had to know how to answer the phone. We used to kid him a lot about this one time when some ambassador called... the Hungarian Ambassador's office or something. One of us answered the phone and made a mistake. We answered "Goldsmith Shoes," and we should have answered "Jewish Renaissance Foundation." We laughed then, and I still give myself a chuckle when I remember this.

He did all of this "out of a shoebox." He really didn't have any offices or staff or anything else; he worked the beginnings of this whole charity out of the shoe store.

At the end he started to get ready to close the store. We were having a closing sale. I don't know where he was; he was out. We were selling shoes for a dollar a pair and whatever, just to get rid of them. The store was a blooming mess. Women were coming in from all over. We were throwing boxes and shoes...and laughing. A couple of guys said, "We can't have all these shoeboxes around," so we threw all the stuff into the back room. Alan came in and said, "What's going on?" We said, "Go in the back." He goes in the back, and the whole back room is just full of empty shoeboxes.

So "the guys"—that's what we call ourselves—helped Alan finish up with the shoe business while he was moving into the Foundation's business. He was so dedicated to his goal. So we watched from the sidelines, and the Foundation kept getting bigger and bigger. My G-d, look what he's accomplished.

* * *

63

Another Back Room Story

*A*nother moment ripped right out of a Marx Brothers movie occurred with a woman who is a longtime friend of mine and of the Jewish Renaissance Foundation. She's a former board member for The Boys & Girls Club of Perth Amboy. I knew Yvonne Lopez when she was still in school, around 1975. I was coaching at the high school when she attended. After her graduation, she began working at the bank that became Wachovia.

In the beginning years of Foundation business, one of the ways we actively sought start-up money involved contacting local banks. Yvonne and I crossed paths because of this. I had contacted a local bank about funding for our projects. They sent their representative, Yvonne Lopez.

That's how Yvonne came to walk into my shoe store. Her visit was my opportunity to present the Foundation's work to a possible funding source.

I wanted to make a good impression. And I especially wanted to highlight the scope and impact of the charitable work we were undertaking.

The back room of my store was becoming the "office" for the Foundation. It was a small room, but served its purpose well since the walls were covered with shelves from floor to ceiling. Naturally, those shelves had once *only* been packed with shoeboxes. But, the shoes were making way for boxes and boxes of medicine. That room was the only place we had for the steady accumulation of medical supplies. As we amassed more and more supplies, medicine, pharmaceutical samples, and equipment were piled all over that room. The day Yvonne visited, we were in the midst of planning an overseas medical mission and had stockpiled an even bigger cache of medicines and other supplies than usual. The place was overloaded.

When Yvonne walked into Goldsmith Shoe Store, I was primed to show our Foundation in the best light possible. This was a tremendously important moment. I felt that I had one chance to impress the bank's representative with the growing scope of the Foundation's upcoming projects. I was chomping at the bit to bring her right into the Foundation's world. So, it was a very natural inclination on my part to move her from the shoe store into the Foundation "office." Almost as soon as she entered and our introductions and pleasantries were finished, I invited her into the back of the store. I was very eager, and it showed.

Yvonne gave me a sideways glance and a shot me a suspicious look that said something like, "Are you nuts? What are you up to?" I could tell that she thought my invitation was very weird. But, I guess my "good guy" personality showed through the awkward invitation, and she went with me. When we crossed into that storeroom, she was instantly overwhelmed with the ceiling-high stockpile of supplies we had amassed for our overseas missions.

It's been a standing joke with us since then...something like "Yeah, Alan tried to lure me into the back of his store." We always get a laugh out of remembering those beginning steps. And yes, her bank gave us one of our first grants.

* * *

64

Yvonne Lopez's Comments (2010)

*A*lan and I have a fourteen-year relationship. It's very personal; it's very professional. He calls me Alice, and I call him Ralph...like The Honeymooners. I adore him; he's like a big brother. In fact, he, his wife, and I have a great, close relationship. Fourteen years is a long time. Longer than most marriages survive (laughing).

I've been a banker for twenty years. Fourteen years ago, I worked for Cores State Bank (now Wachovia). I was in the Community Development Department. My manager approached me one day and told me, "We received a phone call from a Dr. Goldsmith. He's starting up this really interesting organization in Perth Amboy. We want you to check him out. Go meet with him, and learn a bit more about this organization. Get a feel for whether or not his mission and vision is in alignment with our company's values and our foundation-giving guidelines."

I went to the shoe store and met Alan. Alan is very charismatic, always with a great smile. We were chatting in the shoe store about the Jewish Renaissance Foundation and how he had just submitted his paperwork to receive his 501(c)3.

He had a table, just a table, that was designated just for the Jewish Renaissance Foundation administrative work. He shared a phone line with the customers for shoes. Alan was telling me the story of the Foundation, and at one point he told me, "Let's go in the back room, I want to show you something back there." And I remember saying to myself, "I don't think so!" (Laughing) It's a cute story; it's the truth. No, he said, "Really, I have something to show you." He opened the door, and there was a storage room originally reserved for shoes, and it was full of medical supplies.

I got hooked. With that vision, I got hooked...and here I am fourteen years later.

Cores State Bank was the first company to provide him with a grant. We provided him with a five thousand dollar seed grant to get him started. We had huge faith and trust in him.

Fast forward to today...when I look at what's happened...I believe Wachovia just granted the Foundation around eight hundred thousand dollars. There's a legacy there of relationship building and partnership. I've been on the board of the Jewish Renaissance Foundation from the beginning. I've been there forever. It feels like fourteen hundred years (laughing).

* * *

65

Shoelaces And Heartstrings

When speaking about the beginnings of the Foundation in the rear of my little shoe store, I need to round out that part of my story by explaining a bit more about the lunchtime group we called "The Gang." The word "gang" has such horrid connotations, but that's what we called ourselves. It's just that we were a harmless "gang." We were not just a group of guys. Our connections went (and still go) well beyond just "a gathering of friends." Meeting for lunch every day, our little group epitomized the depth of the heartstrings, friendship, and small-town love that paved the pathway of my life.

These guys arrived every day, making this shoe store an even bigger element of my life. This store was much more than just a place, or a source of income, or a building. Of course, thinking about the shoe store invariably brings smiles and tears, because my father and I spent so much time there together. And, of course, the first steps of the Jewish Renaissance

Foundation also came to life in the little back room. But there's more. There are the "guys." This place was almost like an old-fashioned barbershop. You know, the kind you see in movies about "the olden days." It was a place of gossip, tales, talk, laughter, local chatter, good friends, and (of course) that special group of guys. These were the guys who kept the same chairs from floating off the floor day after day. The guys who gave weight to the chairs and even more weight to our deep friendships.

At lunchtime the same three or four guys would come in every day. They could always be counted on to arrive for our daily chat. It was our routine. They were funny. We'd chew over politics, tell jokes, stories, and (of course) rag on each other, much to everyone's enjoyment. They delighted in giving me a hard time about my PhD. Every once in a while, the topic of that degree surfaced in the midst of a wild conversation. Someone would invariably remind me that they thought the initials stood for "piled high and deep." Another favorite joke was to ask me why I needed a PhD to sell shoes. "Is the job so hard?" they'd ask. I can still hear the gales of laughter behind those cracks. We had such fun. And, yes, shoes did get sold.

My old football coach, Ray Geneski, was one of the regulars. Another member of the group was George Pucci, who was very involved with local politics. He was a great guy, very open, very friendly. Two other guys from the neighborhood who worked around the area always stopped in: Marty Clawens and James Reed. Instead of going "out" to lunch they came "in" to my shoe store, "The State Street Gang."

We were serious in our attachment to one another. We even had plaques made commemorating our status in this group. No kidding, real plaques that we hung up. Each plaque carried a "member's" nickname. We all had them, silly names that reflected our role in the gang and our affection for each other. We laughingly accused Ray Geneski of having a cloud that followed him always raining on his parade. So he was known to all on his plaque as "Black Cloud Geneski." I guess we all had nothing better to do at lunchtime than to spend it together. It was wonderful. The guys loved coming into my shoe store to give each other a hard time and laugh like kids. No topic was off limits, so we hashed and rehashed local politics, ongoing neighborhood dramas, the ups and downs in our friends' lives, and old times. We all felt that it was material for a great sitcom. Maybe I could have been the next Archie Bunker or Al Bundy, only more accepting of all people, in the first case, and lots smarter, in the second!

Telling this story now about George Pucci tugs at my heart, but also brings gales of laughter. Pucci loved sharp, costly clothes and top-of-the-line expensive shoes. He was a regular clotheshorse. He didn't usually shop in my store, since I handled more moderately priced shoes. But, once, he bought a really sharp pair from me. They were slip-on shoes, with a snazzy wing-tip design and a tassel on each instep. Pucci absolutely loved those shoes; in fact, he never took them off.

Since he was in and out of my store nearly every day, I had an untold number of occasions to see him in these shoes. One day he came into the store and pointed at his favorite shoes. "Goldy," he said, "the tassel fell off my shoe. What can you do?" I could see that he was upset about his favorite pair of shoes. He should have known how this was going to turn out, with all the joking that was a constant between us. All the guys were watching as I said, "Put your foot up, and let me take a look at it." So he puts up the shoe without the tassel. I laughed and said, "No, no, not that one. Give me the other foot, the one that has the tassel." He brought the other shoe up. I looked at it, grabbed the tassel, and pulled it off. "Now you have two matching shoes." We laughed so hard, we were screaming. The other guys were falling off their chairs.

Two weeks later Pucci came into the store with another complaint about those beloved shoes of his. He said, "Goldy, look at these shoes, the soles ... they're laughing at me." Those soles were flapping. I said, "Go take them to Tony the shoemaker; he'll fix them up." Tony did fix them and stopped those soles from flapping loose. The guys had a great laugh that day, too.

Two years later, when George Pucci passed away at age seventy-six, every one of us was at the wake. His son, who was our age, had him buried in those shoes...his favorite shoes ...without the tassels.

* * *

66

Ray Geneski's Comments

We still meet every day, even now...I mean the guys from the store. In fact, I just got back from lunch with them.

Today, the Gang consists of the guys that are left from the shoe store days...Marty Clawens, Jim Reed, and some additions since then, like Jay Ziznewski. Jay jumped onboard since the Foundation days. Jay was Alan's football teammate from high school. They still kid around about who was the better football player.

Sometimes it gets a little out of hand. Now I kid them all; now they're not afraid of me. Now they talk back to me. Of course, they're all sixty years old now, and I'm seventy-four. It's really great to have these kids I coached, as friends, still part of my life. It's really another amazing thing.

Alan's a character; he really is. What a good-natured guy he is. He still has that "can-do" spirit from the days of the football victories. He always worked *hard, and he still does. That doesn't mean we're not having fun. We are. The back and forth kidding really makes the day great. Alan's serious about the Foundation. He applies all his energies to what he's created, to helping wherever he can.*

* * *

67

Shoes—Part Of G-d's Plan

*I*always felt (and still do) that G-d is planning all this, and I'm just along for the ride. That shoe store, for instance, was just another part of the plan.

It takes so much work to run a store. Ask anyone who runs a business and has to watch the bottom line, while juggling every tiny detail that enters into working a business and trying to make a profit so he and his family can eat. Not only did I have to keep the window displays current, I had to order shoes in time for each season, attend trade shows, organize stock within the store, keep the books and orders in some kind of regular system and current…in short, more than full-time work for two people.

When I entered the business with Dad in 1980, I took it upon myself to update the bookkeeping and spent inordinate amounts of time working on an online procedure. This process was all-consuming. My dad and I worked side by side, six days a week, for nearly four years. When I lost him, not only was I emotionally bereft but running the store alone was proving to be a job for Hercules. I realized what a tremendous load running the store by himself had been for my dad and what huge sacrifices he made for our family. I needed help, and I received it. As I have often said, everything I ever needed, when I needed it, came from above.

Times were changing, and the creation of malls, plus the migration to the suburbs, was affecting us all. Sales were down, and our clientele was disappearing. A really large store, Slobodian Shoes, closed. Two of their best and most seasoned salespeople came over and joined me at Goldsmith Shoe Store around 1986. That's when George Brodsky and Mickey Wolfson joined the Goldsmith team. The arrival of George and Mickey brought a lot of business. Clientele from that old and respected shoe store came with them. Slobodian's had a large and loyal following.

It was really wonderful, too, that George had known my father and knew Annie's father, and incidentally was about the same age my father would have been. Having George and Mickey was a tremendous boost to business, and to me, personally. They had been in the shoe business for a lifetime; I had been in the business a handful of years. Their arrival was more than welcome and very comfortable and comforting. In a very real way, George was like a surrogate father to me. Not only were his and Mickey's help and knowledge a godsend, but it was like working with family again. We worked well together, and they took some of the heavy burden off my back. Our acquaintances developed into very strong friendships. When George passed away, it was like my adopted dad had passed. I helped his family with the funeral arrangements and brought food to the *shiva*– nothing less than I would do for family. He is buried very close to the spot where my parents are laid to rest.

* * *

68

A Good And Loving Woman

When I say that family is a motivation in my story, that the love and support of my family was one powerful impetus in my movement along the path my life has taken, I must highlight my beloved wife. Her love, her support, and her sacrifice have played a huge part in the possibilities for success of this brand new undertaking.

When I closed the store and sold off everything, all we had to begin the Foundation's work was a small grant. Some people look at the scope of our work now and think, "Oh, this was easy." It wasn't. Money did not come flying in, even when the purpose and ideas were noble and needed. When I began focusing exclusively on the Foundation's work, to say we were working on a shoestring budget would have been a gross understatement. That's where Annie's support and heart came to be more important than ever.

Until the Foundation really started to grow, Annie kept our little family afloat. My wife gets credit for those first years when we were really struggling. She was teaching school. We all know that teachers aren't the highest paid professionals. We were making do on Annie's salary and the small amount of money I brought in. That was the time when she really played a crucial part in helping build the Foundation. Until we really started to grow—and it took more time than I care to remember—Annie's salary was one of the very important cogs in our little machine. We kept chugging along because of her help.

The track record for nonprofits is not impressive or auspicious. Maybe one in a thousand startup nonprofits make it. The rest die quickly; one to seven years is the average span. Having sold everything from the shoe store, and putting my full-time work into our little effort, Annie became one of the strong legs of our support base.

* * *

69

Ann Goldsmith's Comments

*A*lan was going to run the shoe store full-time with his father. The dynamics of the town changed drastically. The shoe store was not a high-end fashion shoe store. It dealt with older clientele who needed comfortable, sturdy shoes. It involved a lot of correct fitting, those kind of shoes. Our customers kept coming back. This type of customer was a dying breed. Over the years the business started to falter more and more. We were, at a point, living off my teaching salary. I couldn't understand the emotional part of it. It was Alan's grandfather's, then his dad's, now it was his.

I was teaching school, and because it was in the same town, I could run over on my lunch break. When you're in that kind of a business, it's a walk-in trade. The times when people are not in the store, what do you do in these businesses? It became a setting for "The Guys." They hung out. You'd have a bunch of people sitting and discussing city politics, you know, with a lot of time on their hands.

One day, I remember walking in, and Alan's in the back room. There are papers, there's this other person, and I said, "What are you doing?" He said, "I have this idea for the Foundation." In all honesty, I thought he was insane. Literally insane. (Laughing)

Because over the years he's come up with some real doozies of ideas. "Okay," I thought, "here we go again." I never would have thought in a thousand years… when I look today…at where this is…the number of people who work for him, what he does, that this would ever be what it is now from starting in the shoe store, and Alan saying, "I've got this idea!"

* * *

Part II

"One People, One Heart"

The Business Of Heart

70

A Whole Lot Of Heart— And Not Much More

My wife's cousin was an accountant. So when I closed the doors on Goldsmith Shoe Store for good, in 1997, I tapped family—who else?—to get me up and running in my first steps into the nonprofit world. The learning curve was very steep! Annie's cousin helped us by working on the 501(c)3, a designation given by the federal government to nonprofit organizations for tax-exempt status. This was just the first of the bureaucratic hurdles I was going to learn about and face. I needed to pay legal fees, not an unsubstantial amount, to get the corporation up and running. Thus, I dived headfirst into the adventure of establishing a nonprofit.

I went to the doctors whom I knew personally. My relationships went way back with these people. We were—here's that word again—friends. How important my friends have always been, and here, beginning this tremendous project, friends played an important beginning role. These first doctors involved in the health fairs reached out to other doctors they knew. Some of these pioneers are still on the board of the Jewish Renaissance Foundation, such as Dr. Howard Novick, Dr. Michael Hymanson, and Dr. Judy Amorosa. We started a classic geometric progression. The power of giving started fanning out even in those early days. Grandpa Hymie's spark was on the move.

At that time I made a contact at Eastern Dental. This corporation had dental centers all over New Jersey and the United States. Since we were only working in Middlesex County at the time, that's where I asked them for help. They provided free dental treatment for our charity patients. We were again making headway. Their work came totally from the heart. When the doctors began to see the kind of impact they and we could have donating little bits of time, more of them came onboard. The donation of just a little bit of their time had such a growing impact on the public's health and well-being. I went to the Perth Amboy Board of Education and recruited their help. They gave me the use of a school gymnasium. We set up tables there, and organized a central point to gather the doctors. Patients came. The county participated and was able to offer vaccinations at this central point that became a gathering place for aid.

We started to see enormous results. Near the beginning, we actually saw around seven hundred to eight hundred people in one day. They were able to see a doctor, receive some care, and get advice on getting and staying well, all for free. We started to receive support from all quarters. Banks jumped on board, more doctors and dentists became involved, and various HMOs joined with us. The possibilities grew, our outreach grew, and our vision took flight.

* * *

71

Rainmaker

My job as president of the Jewish Renaissance Family of Organizations is to oversee all the corporations that fall under our umbrella. I make sure they run smoothly and that all our corporations are communicating. It's crucial to the effectiveness of our organizations that everybody knows what the others are doing.

Today, the forty-eight-thousand-square-foot Jewish Renaissance Medical Center on Hobart Street is the heart of the Jewish Renaissance Family of Organizations. Before that center took shape, we only had a tiny medical center with four exam rooms. We continue to reach into other communities to bring needed medical care. As I become aware of more needs, I try to forge a pathway to get funding to launch programs for the specific group in need. The search for funding is ongoing. Rainmaking is a full-time job.

Now the Jewish Renaissance Family of Organizations encompasses many entities. Each corporation is forged to offer help in a specific area. Each one has a separate board of directors, its own tax ID number, EIN number, and separate payroll. Right now we are serving large numbers of people needing medical and dental assistance, reaching out to children in afterschool programs, offering camps to the children with special needs, trying to make a difference to low-income families who need housing, and attempting to help young men and women who need to finish high school, want to learn a trade, and can learn to build and renovate those houses. And that's just a portion of the Jewish Renaissance Family of Organization's programs.

* * *

72

The Foundation's Growth

The Jewish Renaissance Foundation is an entity that germinated from the tiny seed of an idea sown, rooted, and grown in the back of the shoe store on State Street, and took on proportions that are bigger than even I imagined at that time. The incipient moments were indeed small and somewhat inconsequential, but they took place one after another in that back room. No matter how you look at those first attempts in our charitable work, they look tenuous and tiny compared to what we are accomplishing today, and to the places the Jewish Renaissance Family of Organizations reaches.

When I incorporated the Foundation in 1996, and started moving in the direction we march today, I kept my focus on two things: the love, power, and guidance the Almighty had supplied to me throughout my entire life, and my desire to help my fellow man. Those two tenets formed the basis, the bedrock, and (if I can be permitted a small touch of hubris) the covenant that I established with myself, G-d, and humanity, when we took those first steps to becoming a Foundation in every sense of that word.

* * *

73

Sandy Cross's Comments

(CEO FOR THE JEWISH RENAISSANCE FOUNDATION
YOUTH BASED SERVICES PROGRAM)

*T*he Jewish Renaissance Foundation has really strong roots here in Perth
Amboy. The idea of giving back is so important. We try to instill that
in the kids that we work with in our programs. Community service is
such an integral part of a lot of the youth programs that we run here at the Jewish
Renaissance Foundation. That idea of giving back is so important. Take a look at
the Jewish Renaissance Foundation's mission statement.

We have done so much, and so quickly, which is one of the things about what
Alan has done. When you think about our existence being fourteen or fifteen years,
maybe twenty years, when you add the years Alan was thinking about what he
wanted to do.

We're a very young agency compared to other agencies, and we have done a heck of a lot of growing in the past five years. Sometimes the naysayers say things like, "How did they get to where they are so fast?" Kids have a name for that. They call them "The Haters." Out there, "The Haters" see you doing well, and they hate you. I come across these "Haters" all the time.

One time I responded this way to someone who doubted our sincerity, one of these "Haters." He actually said something to me like, "Do you even have a mission, or do you just kind of go out there and do whatever you can get?" I said to him, "Our mission says that we must respond to the needs of our neighbors and share our talents. Do you know who our neighbors are?" This man just looked at me. I added, "My neighbor is not just the man who lives next door. My neighbor is the town that I live in. My neighbor is the people in the county that I live in and the state that I live in. So when we see a need in our neighbor, we try to meet that need with the talents that we have."

This mission is very scriptural. That's my favorite part of our mission...that we respond to the needs of our neighbors and share our talents and resources. To me that's who we are. We have a talent for working with young people. Then yeah, a lot of our focus is working with young people. As you grow as an agency, you grow in your talents. You see that the gifts you have can help young people and be transferred to help them and their families. That's when you start seeing all the other things you can do.

That's how it was for the Jewish Renaissance Foundation. We started very small to help people get medical services for free. Then we started getting into youth services, mostly geared here in Perth Amboy. Then we got one grant to work with out-of-school youth (sixteen to twenty-four-year olds) whether they graduated from high school or not. Then you find yourself working with their families, and next thing you know, you're providing services for the entire county. Then all of a sudden you're like, "Whoa! We're actually providing services for some people outside our county," which is what the medical center now does. So initially our neighbors might have been just the people in this little area, but because we kept our eyes open to the needs of the people around us, we couldn't help but continue to grow.

That's our motto..."One People, One Heart." By no means am I saying that we're perfect. We have made our mistakes, but we recognize the mistakes we make.

Sometimes having a big heart exposes you to elements you shouldn't expose yourself to as an agency. Some people have been working with the Jewish Renaissance Foundation for quite a few years. I think you have to have a heart for the work that you do in order to stay here, or else you don't fit in. There's a particular environment at Jewish Renaissance Foundation, and if you don't buy into that environment, you can't stay. I am definitely gung-ho Jewish Renaissance Foundation!

* * *

74
What's In A Name?

Before I can recount the tremendous stories that demonstrate the power of giving, stories that demonstrate the strength of *tzedakah* (charity), I need to establish some background and set the record straight. I chose the name for the Jewish Renaissance Foundation based upon my faith and the belief that G-d has been the guide and impetus behind every move I have made in my life. I truly believe that I earned a pass that day I walked away from the car accident, based on the merits of my grandparents' and parents' lives. This miracle was a gift based on my family's virtuous record, definitely not mine. I know in my heart that I was spared because G-d wanted me to walk a path, one that I wasn't aware of yet that devastating night.

I decided then, even as I lay stunned on the side of the road, that since I owed my life to G-d's mercy, that I would work to try to pay back. Since I owed my life to G-d, I wanted to mold and direct my life in gratitude for that. I wanted to dedicate my path to more than just living my own life. I wanted to make this world a better place. At that time I just didn't know how this would occur.

In choosing the "Jewish Renaissance Foundation" as the original name for the organization, I simply wanted to honor the Almighty. The Jewish Renaissance Foundation's doors and programs are open to humanity. The name is personal and special to me. The name reflects my beliefs and my path. Some people have come to me with the suggestion that I change the name. "It's too 'Jewish,'" they say, or, "People will think you're running a religious organization." I'm not so sure that many people believe that to be true once they witness the scope of our work.

In spite of what some people believe about the dimensions of our work, due to the sound of our name, our vital and expanding Foundation serves all people. People who know me, know that I fashion my own life according to the dictates of the Almighty and Jewish law. That doesn't mean our patients need to do that. The Talmud states that all Jews are responsible for one another. I look at that statement, and I choose to stretch and mold it into what I think is good, and holy and appropriate. I apply G-d's law to humanity. I believe we are all responsible for one another. And that's how we direct the programs of the Jewish Renaissance Family of Organizations. Our programs and our works are for humanity…now that's a group we all belong to, isn't it? So the name reflects my beliefs and our work reflects everyone's.

I have seen this narrow point of view about our Foundation's name again and again. I have witnessed more times than I care to remember when people seemed to chafe at the inclusion of the word "Jewish" in our title. In those earlier years, when the Jewish Renaissance Foundation was seeing charity care patients on a much smaller scale than we are capable of now, and we were working hard to gain approval as a Federally Qualified Health Center, this negative feeling appeared again.

The paperwork and bureaucratic tangles were huge. This time-consuming and intricate process was completed one step at a time, with diligence and perseverance. We became the first faith-based Federally Qualified Health Center in the country, and we were so content with the results. One of the government workers, in looking over our stats, said, "Maybe you should change your name to something other than the Jewish Renaissance Medical Center. How about just the Renaissance Medical Center?" I was quite surprised, and asked him, "Why would you even say that?" His answer also surprised me. He said, "People might think it's just for Jewish people." My answer to him satisfied me then, and does so even more now. My response was, "When someone goes to St. Peter's or St. Michael's Hospitals, do you think they think about whether those centers are only for Catholic patients?"

The fact that the Jewish Renaissance Medical Center was the very first faith-based health care center to earn federal status was a huge step. His comments made me even more aware of who we were. When I reflected back on what I went through to get the medical center up and running, the amazing complex legal steps, the grant writing, the forms, talking to and reaching out to countless people, I had that certainty rise up in me again and again. This initiative, this Jewish Renaissance Medical Center, was not just my doing. I only served as G-d's instrument to start this project moving. I only served G-d in constructing this institution that was going to help so many people...so many *different* people. I just couldn't "dis" the Almighty, if you'll permit me the modern expression. I couldn't turn my back on the path I knew I walked, by ignoring the power given to me. I couldn't take my religion and my beliefs out of this undertaking, because I believe that the Almighty has been the engine every step of the way in moving me along this path. My religion and my beliefs form the core of who I am and what I do.

When I finished explaining all of this, the man replied, "I didn't mean it in that respect." He apologized. Looking back, I can honestly say that I have lived and honored the teachings of my grandfathers—two men who taught me that giving is a blessing, and that giving anonymously is an even bigger blessing. "Just put the money under the door, and run away." I guess we've been running away for about fourteen years.

* * *

75
Small World

This tale not only clarifies what we do in the Jewish Renaissance Family of Organizations, but solidifies the concept of how small the world is and how interconnected we all are. Around 2007, eleven years into the Jewish Renaissance Foundation's work, a young woman named Victoria Avalishvili contacted the Jewish Renaissance Foundation. She had been frantically searching for help for her critically ill father. This man had been a famous Russian Olympic soccer player and still lived in the Republic of Georgia. The state of medicine in that country did not even begin to meet his needs. He had advanced colon cancer.

As a last ditch effort to save her father, Victoria had been searching online for any means to help him. While scouring the Internet, she eventually typed "Jewish and Medical." The search engine presented her with the name of the Jewish Renaissance Foundation and Medical Center.

She contacted the Jewish Renaissance Foundation, and thus began our connection.

When Victoria located our Foundation, she sent me a very detailed e-mail about her father's life and his threatening illness. I learned about her father's fame and the glory he had helped bring to the Russian nation as a member of the 1980 Olympic soccer team. Moses Avalishvili had been the only Jewish soccer player on that team. He was a first-class player. She explained to me that the Russian government knew they had a victorious team going into those Olympic games, but they had one big problem with Moses. The "powers that be" wanted him to change his name. His obvious Jewish identity bothered the Russian government. They wanted him to adopt a name that didn't sound Jewish for this historical moment when the Russian soccer team was set to explode onto the very public world sports stage.

That news hit me as if I'd been swatted with a two-by-four. Here was a man who, like me, had experienced a life where sports was his axis. To become a champion, sports must be your central focus every day. That was true for me during many years, and obviously was for him, too. We also shared another set of experiences. He had been asked to hide his Jewish identity for other people's comfort and satisfaction, just as I had been asked to remove the word "Jewish" from the title I had chosen for the nonprofit I was forming. He was being asked to hide his identity in a nation that did not value its Jewish citizens. He refused, as I had. These similarities in our lives created a strong feeling of kinship in me.

When Victoria explained to me how sick her father was, and described the critical stage of his disease, her story grabbed me by the heart. I decided that the Jewish Renaissance Foundation would help find the lifesaving care her father needed.

She flew her father to the US, and our team took over. We brought him to the Cancer Institute of New Jersey, in New Brunswick, where he received top-notch medical care. Victoria's fortuitous involvement with the Jewish Renaissance Foundation saved Moses's life. He eventually was well enough to return to his home in the Republic of Georgia, but came back about a year later for continued treatment of his cancer. These treatments and surgeries, although quite severe due to the advanced nature of his disease when he first came to our doctors' attention, enabled him to live three more years in relative comfort. The Jewish Renaissance Foundation's involvement with this family was a factor in our Foundation's becoming better known outside our country's borders.

Victoria had connections to the first lady of the Republic of Georgia. She was instrumental in arranging our contact to Ms. Sandra Roelofs, the wife of the president of that Republic. Ms. Roelofs' office contacted me in 2008. She asked for my help in bringing doctors and medicine to her people. The Republic of Georgia was in desperate need of help. Updated medical care was long overdue in that part of the world. The Georgian medical system was in a shambles. They were still using one hospital that had been in use during World War II, and was totally unsuited for their present needs. The breakup of the Soviet Union left that area totally unprepared for the present, let alone the future. And it was the ordinary people who were in the most desperate need of basic medical care.

We anticipated sending doctors and medicines to Georgia and began drawing up plans to reach out to them. The Jewish Renaissance Foundation had begun to reach farther and farther into international waters.

Ms. Roelofs traveled to Perth Amboy to see our medical center. She wanted to see firsthand how a progressive community health center was created and run. We showed her the entire facility. She met with our doctors and nurses, and witnessed firsthand how our most needful citizens were benefiting from first-rate care. She and I shared her visit and the story of our collaboration with the media, in a press conference. We had a very fruitful meeting and established a bond that will continue into the future.

* * *

76

Goldy At The United Nations

I met a man named Ben Shalom at a fundraiser in New York around 2004. He was a Goodwill Ambassador, trying to create harmony and peace in the world, and had been honored by the Pope. We started discussing ways to help the underserved communities here in New Jersey and in other countries, as well as ways of honing our abilities to serve these needful groups in the world's population. He thought that it would be beneficial for me to work within the structure of the United Nations. And he introduced me to the president of the Intergovernmental Institution for the Use of Micro-Algae Spirulina Against Malnutrition (IIMSAM).

I was named Goodwill Ambassador to IIMSAM through the United Nations Economic and Social Council in 2004. Through our Operation Lifeline International, we have already traveled to nations in need and will continue to send doctors and medicines to underdeveloped countries or others experiencing difficulties. My status as Goodwill Ambassador means that the medical missions I lead to foreign nations will all travel under the protection of the United Nations, with diplomatic immunity.

In 2007 I met with the people from IIMSAM. I was named as a senior adviser. That international group is instrumental in utilizing the micro-algae spirulina to prevent malnutrition worldwide. (Spirulina contains enormous amounts of phytonutrients.) So now the Jewish Renaissance Foundation is in a position to help in the fight to lessen the effects of mal-nutrition and hunger.

I have accepted this title, not for me, but for our organization. Our Foundation achieves more credibility with this connection. I now have the ability to help a lot more people all over the world. The connection to IIMSAM broadens the scope of our work.

In September of 2007 I spoke at a luncheon at the United Nations building on a day when the General Assembly was meeting. The Mission to El Salvador and The Global Center organized the get-together. They hosted a luncheon on the fourth floor of the U.N. in order to address the issues of water purification and combating malnutrition. Numerous dignitaries were present, among them five presidents, members of UNICEF, repre-sentatives of WHO (the World Health Organization), and several ambassa-dors from Central and South America. The co-founder of this organization, Dr. Gilda Glasinovich, was also present. When the ambassadors finished their work in the assembly, they were invited to attend our speech and luncheon. What we were able to carry out that day very unusual.

While I was in the U.N. Delegate Lounge I met and chatted with ambassadors, counselors, and ministers. While speaking to the ambassador to Italy and delegates from IIMSAM, an Iraqi prince walked over to express his desire that I travel to Fallujah, Iraq with our medical teams. They were in need of assistance in treating their children and were interested in addressing preventative and ongoing medical care. It seemed to be a perfect opportunity to make a small step forward in Arab-Jewish relations. I told them that I could probably convince my doctors to go if they guar-anteed that security issues would be addressed and taken care of. He told us that they would supply security for this mission. However, the prince said, "There is one thing. You can't bring any of your Jewish doctors." I was absolutely taken aback. I actually found myself speechless, grasping for words. What nerve, I thought. But I was too shocked to speak. I couldn't even make my mouth form the words, I was so surprised by his statement.

Finding myself at a loss for words is not a regular occurrence! Before I spat out one word, one of the ambassadors jumped in. "How can you even think of telling this to the director of a Jewish organization? Aren't you aware that Dr. Goldsmith is Jewish?" The prince stammered and retorted that he hadn't really meant anything bad by saying that, to which the ambassador said, "Dr. Goldsmith will not be bringing any doctors to your country with that stipulation." It was better coming from him than from me. I probably would not have used such diplomatic language. I was furious. This man just turned and walked away. Such chutzpah at the U.N.

* * *

77

Operation Hope

ARABS AND JEWS

One of the programs of the Jewish Renaissance Family of Organizations, called Operation Hope, is geared for high school kids who are in danger of being lost in the system, dropping out, and falling through the cracks of life. Operation Hope gives these kids a chance to pick up the pieces of their young lives and get back onto an education and success track. We offer them a chance to finish high school with a GED, and we offer them vocational training. A very strong component of this program is to help these young men and women find a functional and economically viable place for themselves in society.

Dr. Goldsmith with a group of local teens from Jewish Renaissance Foundation's "Operation Hope", which was designed to help troubled teens earn their GED's and get vocational training, 2002.

A Muslim girl, about seventeen years old, was one of the young women taking advantage of this program. I found her to be bright, sweet, and cordial. She had a very friendly character and was respectful of her peers and teachers. During one conversation I had with her, we talked about our Jewish-Muslim connection. I asked her if she didn't feel strange coming to a program that had "Jewish" in its name. Her answer was straightforward and honest. She said, "I heard so many good things about you. This is a good program, and my parents and I wanted to participate." I told her that the directors had told me so many good things about her, too.

Then 9/11 happened. It's still hard to think about that horrible event and those viciously difficult days of the aftermath. I know a number of people personally who were impacted by the death of loved ones. The entire world went a bit crazy after this terrible attack. On a local level, we saw more acts of bravery, selflessness, and heroism than we had ever imagined possible. The best in Americans gushed forth from the hearts and souls of nameless hoards of every nationality, religion, ethnicity, and political bent. People rushed to Ground Zero and nearby communities to offer any help they could. Humanity had a moment to shine amid this senseless carnage.

At the same time, some fringe elements found the opportunity ripe to foment and spread vicious racism and prejudice. American Muslims felt themselves under attack. Mercifully, most of this danger never manifested itself in outrage and violence, but the sniveling cowardly evil of prejudice once again stood up to be counted. American Muslims felt themselves besieged by diatribes and invectives; hatred circulated among some fringe groups. People's ignorance once again showed its true colors, very much like the darkest days of World War II, when the same kind of fear caused the marginalization and incarceration of Japanese-Americans and the fear of German-Americans. American Muslims were distrusted and feared.

This young Muslim girl and her family felt this fear and anger most directly. Their religion dictated that the women wear head scarves at all times to display their modesty. The women in this young woman's family followed this tradition. It was, therefore, very easy to single them out. It was in these highly charged days in the aftermath of the destruction of the two World Trade Center towers that the family became the targets of mindless racist-inspired violence.

While riding in their car, some young ignorant people started yelling and throwing stones at them. One projectile broke through the window, sending pieces of glass into the eye of our student's sister. The child wasn't hurt very badly, but she did need medical care. Our student was almost finished with the classwork and testing needed to get her GED. She was so close to reaching her goal. Her parents, very understandably, were horrified at the racism and hateful outburst they had experienced and were frightened for the safety of the family. The parents made the decision to send the children to live and study in Trinidad.

I felt hurt and horrified that ignorant people could carry out such a violent attack based on someone wearing different clothing. I have a personal understanding of racism. No Jew who wears a *kippah* (*yarmulke*) as I do, has escaped this negative emotion. I have noticed it palpably, even when people say nothing. Yet people have said things to me. Again and again I have been advised to "hide" my Jewishness, to lose the *kippah*, and to remove the word "Jewish" from our Foundation's name. This family chose to wear their head coverings. I truly understood their dilemma and their fears.

I offered this Muslim girl lodging in my home. I wanted her to have the opportunity to complete her studies and find her footing again. In the spirit of the work I do, the faith I have, and the legacy of my family, I offered this young woman's parents the option of allowing her to finish the high school degree while residing with Annie and me. My wife and I have ample room in our Spotswood home. I told them that she could remain with us until she finished her GED, and then we would send her to be with her family.

I even laughingly mentioned that it would be so simple for the three of us to exist under the same roof; the dietary laws that Annie and I follow are basically the same for the Muslim young lady. She liked the idea, and she brought our offer to her parents. We dialogued with them. They thanked us, but turned down the offer. They felt it would be better for her to attend a Madrasah in Trinidad. This is the type of understanding that is possible when we look past labels, clothing preferences, and religion to understand each other's hearts. We're all G-d's children; why can't people see and respect that? This again was the legacy of my grandparents reaching over the years to touch me and my heart today.

THE JEWISH HARLEY DAVIDSON

The story of another one of our Operation Hope participants underscores the power inherent in and the necessity of reaching out to our youth. Jaimie was an eighteen-year-old Mexican lad who fit nobody's definition of a success story. In fact, he looked like Hollywood's version of trouble. If Jaime were walking toward someone on the sidewalk, that person would probably run across the street until Jaimie passed. This young man was really big and enormously husky. That alone gave him a menacing appearance. He also sported rings all over his face; rings poked out of his cheeks, nose, and eyes, and he wore his hair in a long ponytail. He was an alarming sight. What you couldn't see at first glance was his gentle, charming nature. In fact, he was the gentlest person I had ever met.

Jaimie worked with us through the Operation Hope program. He earned his GED, with our help and support. In addition to the impetus we tried to give him in setting his goals and meeting them, we made it clear to him that he needed to follow his dreams. And Jaimie's clear and focused dream was to become a Harley Davidson mechanic.

Jaimie earned his GED, and we hired him as a facilities person in our office building, The Proprietary House. This gave him the cash flow that was necessary to continue moving toward his goals. This wonderful fellow looked on us as his second family.

What does a family do but put every effort behind a "son" to help him further his dreams? We helped him apply to the Harley Davidson school in Colorado, where he would get the Harley mechanic training he so wanted. That school also offered him other types of training. He won acceptance there, and we gave him a thousand dollar scholarship, funding his trip and lodgings. The end result was that Jaimie graduated.

With this success behind him and his new credentials as a mechanic buoying his life, Jaimie returned to Perth Amboy. He came to see us, thanked us for our support and belief in him, and told me he wanted to do something special for us. He wanted me to tell him what he could do, what he could give us as thanks. So, I told him, in my joking way, I wanted a Jewish Harley Davidson. He asked me, "What's a Jewish Harley Davidson?" I said, "It's a Harley Davidson with training wheels!" He got a big laugh out of that.

The next time he came to see me, he brought me exactly what I had requested...a model Harley Davidson with tiny training wheels. One of the cutting edge classes he took at the Harley facility involved training in the use of lasers to cut and shape metal. Putting that new skill to great use, Jaimie gave us our gift. A beauty it was, too!

Jaimie was now set and ready to enter his chosen profession. He was a bona fide Harley Davidson mechanic. Even better, he was also trained and prepared to work on other cycles, too. Jaimie was set to earn very satisfactory wages; good mechanics earn good money. This young man could now take his place in the world.

* * *

78

Mezuzah Power

I had the privilege to be honored by the Hadassah in November 2009. The gathering was quite large, with over three hundred fifty people present. The evening was a dual pleasure; I shared the honors that evening with the first ordained female rabbi. The rabbi received her ordination way back in 1972, which was quite revolutionary at the time. It always is when women, or members of any minority, step out of the established pattern and create a new one.

I have received quite a few honors and awards in the last few years. It sometimes makes me a bit uneasy, because I was taught that the best way to give is to give anonymously. However, the realities of the nonprofit and of marketing make it necessary to keep our name in the public eye. But it's somewhat ironic that this was the first award given to me by a Jewish group. I have received over thirty-five awards from so many wonderful groups that work to further humankind themselves. The NAACP, the Salvation Army...but this was my very first award from a Jewish source. My wife and I joined Hadassah that evening. So, now I am an associate member.

The wonderful women Annie and I met that evening offered their agency's aid to the Foundation. "What," they asked, "can we do?" I told them a story, another wonderful anecdote, from so many heartwarming and endearing moments that have occurred within the outreach of the Foundation's work. This incident resonated strongly with me when it occurred. When the Jewish Renaissance Foundation was beginning to offer outpatient services, we existed on a very small scale. Our little medical center only had four examination rooms. I had affixed a *mezuzah* to the doorjamb of each exam room. A *muzuzah* is a small tube or box containing a parchment inscribed with biblical passages. Jews are commanded to place a *mezuzah* on the upper right side of the doorpost of the home. We felt that the doors to the four exam rooms should also carry this blessing. It's a beautiful custom, and we hung them.

Somehow, one of them came unfixed from the door post, and as will happen in a very busy office, it did not go back up quickly. So it just happened that on one particular day, there were three exam rooms with a *mezuzah*, and one without. The Jewish Renaissance Foundation's clients were Hispanic, black, Caucasian, Catholic, Protestant, Jewish— a virtual United Nations of our own.

On this particular day, a Hispanic woman was being ushered into an exam room to await her doctor. The nurse directed her into the one room where the *mezuzah* was missing. The patient turned to me and said she wanted to go into another room. When we asked her why, she said with great conviction, "I know what that box means. It's supposed to protect me. I want to go into a room with a box." The nurse led her to another room, one with a *mezuzah*. The patient was content.

When I recounted the story, the room full of Hadassah members began buzzing. All the women loved the story. Discussion ensued, and the group volunteered a superb idea. They decided to undertake a project to collect money to purchase a *mezuzah* for each exam room in the new

Jewish Renaissance Medical Center. I was pleasantly surprised. I had no ulterior motive in sharing that story, other than to express the impact our Foundation has on everyone—all religions, all races, all cultures. I told them the story only to demonstrate the scope of our impact, and to stress that all of us desire similar things. I wasn't fishing for a donation, and I certainly wasn't trolling for *mezuzahs*! But what a wonderful idea it was, one that gave these generous and warmhearted women from Hadassah a meaningful project in support of the Jewish Renaissance Medical Center.

Sometime after that evening, I received an e-mail from this Hadassah chapter. They have undertaken the project with energy and are collecting funds to purchase the *mezuzahs* for our fifty exam rooms. One man's need becomes another man's *mitzvah* (good deed).

* * *

79

Mobile Medicine

After 9/11, we wanted to help more than ever. We already had a crew of doctors and nurses available, and we were ready to help. The problem on that horrid day was they couldn't get into New York City. The injured were being ferried to Jersey City, right across the river from downtown New York. So Jersey City became on off-site medical command center. Communications were a shambles. Cell towers were overloaded, and functioning intermittently. Communications quickly developed into a secondary set of problems. It became obvious that more planning and infrastructure were needed to prepare us to meet the challenges and be effective in the face of a disaster of such tremendous magnitude. We need a more effective system to move medical personnel and equipment into the high-need area, and we also needed a more stable communications system.

Jewish Renaissance Medical Center had already had ideas about mobile medicine, and as an extension, mobile medical command centers. We were taking steps for acquiring a thirty-eight foot mobile medical/dental van. We had applied for a New Jersey state grant for this purpose. When it was awarded to us in 2008, we purchased and outfitted a Winnebago-type van. We now had a movable medical/dental clinic for the people and children who had been going without care in these areas. We currently serve all of Middlesex and Essex Counties.

Our goal became clear as we saw the potential for another use for the medical/dental van. We saw a future for that van to function as a mobile medical command center in the face of an emergency, such as the one we faced on 9/11. We pictured the van containing five stations on each side to treat ten patients at a time. We would have a triage center near the front of the van. From that station the doctors and nurses could either begin to treat some patients right there in the van, or stabilize others for transport to neighboring hospitals. The van would be able to communicate to police and neighboring hospitals through satellite phones that are already installed in the vehicle.

In 2003 we sent our doctors to Israel, where they were trained to treat casualties from nuclear, biological, and chemical warfare. They received hands-on training from top Israeli medical personnel and doctors.

After 9/11, we brought the top specialists from Israel to the United States to participate in the first conference on emergency/terrorist attack/ disaster response. We presented an idea to Middlesex County government officials. We said that if they placed us in the chain of command in the Office of Emergency Management (OEM), we would respond immediately in the event of an emergency or incident. In other words, we would deploy our medical/dental van to the point of most need. The van would be equipped with doctors, emergency-trained specialists, and medical supplies and equipment. In return for this emergency-ready status for our equipment and personnel, they would store the bus at their fire academy. They agreed.

* * *

80

Social Reconnaissance

More and more doctors were joining our ranks in Operation Lifeline, and it was functioning well. But the vision of helping more people and making a bigger impact for the citizens of Middlesex County wouldn't stop nagging at me. It seemed to me that with more effort and work, my vision could grow.

At that long-ago moment, we pictured opening a "one-stop shop," perhaps a community health center, where people could gather in one place and receive care. However, you can't just plop down a community health center anywhere. It has to be established in an area designated as a "medically underserved area or medically underserved population."

Part of the process required us to see how many doctors were already seeing Medicaid patients. The city of Perth Amboy already had one hospital, and that hospital had clinics. That meant Perth Amboy did not qualify as a medically underserved area, but the city did qualify as a medically underserved population. Governor Whitman signed off on this designation. Achieving this qualification took us about a year and a half and was not without costs.

We had all the Health Resources and Services Administration (HRSA) qualifications, we had the state requirements under our belt, and we had a letter of support from the New Jersey Primary Care Association. The Federal Department of Health and Senior Services really wanted to know what was going on in our community. They wanted to know how the demographics were changing, to what degree, and what was going on with the state of health care. Our job became one designed to pull together all the disparate groups from the community.

* * *

81

How Social
Reconnaissance Works

A t the end of 1997, Linda Anderson, who was the head of the charity care program for the state of New Jersey, came to us about participating in a nationwide social reconnaissance study. The Jewish Renaissance Foundation was one of ten agencies selected for this project throughout the United States. Linda met with me on her own time; I believe we met for the first time on a Sunday. She, like so many other people I have met, is so committed to helping others. She has become one of my closest allies and friends. In fact, she'll be going on one of our future overseas medical missions. It turns out that this remarkable woman is a nurse, and she just retired as a colonel from the Army Reserve. She is an invaluable resource and wonderful friend.

The result of this contact was that we were chosen by the federal government to participate in social reconnaissance. We were amazed and pleased to have been selected. Our job was to put together vocal groups consisting of the grassroots of society. The purpose of social reconnaissance is basically to begin to identify problems. Once the identification process begins, the focus turns to studying the barriers that may exist to working with, ameliorating, or solving the issues. And finally, the ultimate goal is to begin to lay out, develop, and present viable solutions. "The powers that be" wanted to know what was going on in our community. So we gathered as many different people and groups as we could. We brought together people from various religious groups, educational groups, nurses from the school district, and hospital staff from all over Middlesex County. The Hispanic presence was growing in our county and within Perth Amboy, so we asked members of the Dominican and Puerto Rican communities to join us. The federal government hired a consultant to work with us. The Department of Senior Services came to participate, and the state sent people.

We met for a whole week. It was a very prolific and information-rich time. We were talking to people, listening to people, and assessing their ideas, needs, wants, and purposes. We studied the needs and looked at the deficiencies they actually experienced, and what they were expecting in terms of change. It was important to ascertain where the money was going and what it was to be used for. This was a huge undertaking that provided a prodigious amount of information. The ultimate recommendation set forth was that the geographical area needed a community health center. Now we had the information we needed to move ahead with my plan to bring a one-stop shop, a medical center, to Perth Amboy's underserved population.

The vision of the Jewish Renaissance Foundation and the findings of the social reconnaissance were basically in sync. We needed a physical plant; we needed a health care center, where all levels of health care could be offered to the people of our community who were in need.

* * *

82

Grant Money

We applied to HRSA in April of 1999 for grant money. We were declined because we didn't yet have a medical center up and running. According to the rules, if the grant is approved, you have to have a center up and running within a hundred twenty days.

There are actually two types of grants. One is a "Look-Alike." A Federally Qualified Health Center Look-Alike designation means a health care organization does not yet have section 330 funding, but gets all the benefits of a Federally Qualified Health Center. These benefits include some very important items, such as charity care funding, and enhanced Medicaid rates. It is usual to open a "Look-Alike" first, abide by all the rules and regulations of the federal government, but without funding. That's one way to get started. After that, it's the time to apply for the "330 grant" funding for a federally funded health care center. So we applied first for the "Look-Alike" status in August of 1999.

We did acquire an earmark from the state for about one hundred fifty thousand dollars to open up a small clinic under the auspices of the Jewish Renaissance Foundation in January of 1999. That constituted a tiny first step. It was quite a long process to get the HMOs on board and to hire a doctor. However, we did it. We were up and running, actually seeing patients by around August of that year.

When we finally received the money to open up that small clinic in Perth Amboy, it opened under the auspices of the Jewish Renaissance Foundation. However, we modeled it after a community health center; that's exactly what we were going to be. At that time our clinic was just a medical clinic. We were not associated yet in any way with the federal government. All we had was that hundred fifty thousand dollars—enough money to open us up, and not much more than that. We plowed ahead for the federal programs. We applied again for both of the grants. We put in applications in August of 1999 (for the "Look-Alike" grant) and closer to the end of 1999, for the "330 grant."

The time frame for applying for the grants only fell at a certain time during the year. The preparation of the grant was a months-long process. When we applied for the "Look-Alike grant" in August 1999, and "the 330 grant" in October 1999, we were competing against other applicants who were also vying for these same grants throughout the entire United States. This included much bigger cities such as San Francisco, Los Angeles, New Orleans, and Atlanta, for example. At the time we were applying, out of the thousands of applications the government received, only forty-five applicants would receive the status of a Federally Qualified Health Center. So the tiny city of Perth Amboy, with its changing immigrant population, was up against huge competition. Here's where my skill of selling shoes came in handy. I was now faced with the most important sales job of my career. We had to sell our senators and congressmen on the need to help us during this process to market ourselves to HRSA. Therefore, we felt it was necessary to write those two grants—one for a "Look-Alike" and one for a "330 grant"—for all the reasons I have mentioned. Being a "330 grantee" meant we would have money coming to us from the "section 330 grant funds." That would give us about six hundred fifty thousand dollars, and we would be off and running.

* * *

83

David And Goliath, Again

We wrote both of these grants, and in November of 1999 we were accepted as a "Look-Alike." By January 2000, we were also accepted as a "330 grantee." This was tremendous and unprecedented. A nonprofit can remain a "Look-Alike" for a couple of years. After that time, it's possible that their status will change and they will move on. This good fortune allowed us to turn our little clinic into a community health center. President Bush's initiative for faith-based health care had come about then.

We had one doctor, and eventually progressed to having more. Every step felt like the biggest victory. I knew, way back then, that our attempts, although quite huge in themselves, were still too meager. We were too small to impact the community in the way I wanted. Our size was a problem, and money was a larger issue. We didn't have the money to build or even purchase a facility.

Little by little, the tiny medical center became more sustainable. I was the CEO at the very beginning. I needed to change my title to that of president so I could oversee the Foundation and the medical center. We only had that one small medical center with four exam rooms. That was all we could afford at this beginning point. The Jewish Renaissance Foundation was growing; we were receiving more grants and moving forward with funding. We needed to look toward the grant option for that funding. Donations alone simply were not a viable option. We exist in a low socioeconomic area, so local donations were not going to make up a substantial portion of our finding.

Slowly, the medical center was becoming more sustainable. The actual physical size of the center was an impediment to growth. With just four exam rooms, there was a very low ceiling for the number of patients we could see and treat. The federal government would have liked us to see more patients, but our tiny size wouldn't allow us to treat more patients.

We were supposed to be servicing patients in the ob-gyn, pediatric, internal medicine, and dental areas. All that in a physical plant of twelve hundred square feet. We needed to be magicians to treat a higher volume of patients in that amount of space. That prompted me to become very active in the search for bigger quarters. I started looking at buildings, as I sought to expand. But, next came a move to the city of Newark, where our paramount concern was delivering quality health care to the children.

* * *

84

Opportunity Serves The Children

*T*he Healthcare Foundation of New Jersey had heard about what I was attempting and what I had actually accomplished in Perth Amboy. They approached us to take a look at their school-based health centers. At that time Newark Beth Israel Hospital was running school-based health centers in Newark. The hospital didn't want to operate them any more. I jumped on this opportunity to provide health care for the children of Newark at no cost for their families or the board of education. I designed a plan where the centers would be self-sufficient. I estimated that we would need financing from the Healthcare Foundation to implement and sustain the centers that first year. After that year, we wouldn't need any money from them. It seemed like a good plan, and Beth Israel loved the idea. They saw the relevance in the program I had developed.

Newark Beth Israel Hospital had been sold to St. Barnabas, and the monies were set up as a trust fund, known as the Healthcare Foundation of New Jersey. They would give out funding to nonprofits and hospitals that would provide medical service to Newark. So when we started out, we received a substantial grant from them to work the same type of program in Newark that I had set up here in Middlesex County.

This collaboration with Beth Israel served more than one purpose. It gave us just what we needed to increase our presence in the community, and truly serve the children of Newark who needed quality access to the health care system.

The establishment of the Jewish Renaissance Medical Center oversight of the school-based health care centers meant that we would be running five pediatric sites in Newark. I established centers for the treatment of students in the participating schools that would also treat anyone up to the age of twenty-one, from the city of Newark and in need of medical care.

By expanding the scope of the population covered and treated in the school-based centers, we established a model for other Federally Qualified Health Centers. Before we took the centers over, Newark Beth Israel was losing money running those school-based sites. The way I had set them up, we expected the clinics to break even. That meant I wouldn't need the grant monies from the Healthcare Foundation. The receipt of a grant from them usually implied that the clinics would run for three years, after which we were expected to be self-sufficient. We seemed to have solved that problem. Also, the state gave Newark Beth Israel six hundred thousand dollars to help run the school-based centers. When the Jewish Renaissance Medical Center took over, that money was granted to us to run those centers. We hope that we'll be able to continue receiving this funding.

* * *

85

Sustainable School-Based Health Care

We worked hard to build a model that would sustain these valuable health resources for our underserved children. We are now able to bill for services because we are a satellite of a Federally Qualified Health Center, which allows the HMOs to reimburse us. When we started the school-based health care centers in Newark, the original plan was to serve school-aged children. But that would not serve enough of the population to make it financially feasible. Once we expanded the population that these school-based centers would serve, including all children in the area up to the age of twenty-one, we had created a model of a Federally Qualified Health Center.

We have initiated more dental care into these school-based centers and have included other aspects of care to better provide for these pediatric patients. But we also offer the services of a psychiatrist at one of the school sites every week, in an effort to provide a more comprehensive health package to Newark's youth. In order to offer an even more complete behavioral health care service to the children, we have placed two licensed clinical social workers (LCSWs) in two other schools for the kids' benefit. We don't feel that this is complete just yet, but until the funding becomes available for full-time coverage, this at least offers this important service to the children of Newark.

We never charge co-pays; the grant pays that charge as well as all lab fees. As with a plan set to work on such a large and widespread scale, some of the centers are underutilized, but most of them are really thriving. We're working with Mayor Cory Booker's administration to expand the school-based health centers' scope and coverage. His office wants us to open medical sites in a special-needs school, plus three others in his city.

The Booker administration would love the Jewish Renaissance Medical Center to service all the schools. We just can't rush into this endeavor. We are working on a systematic plan to increase our presence in the schools. We need to see a minimum number of patients to meet our operating expenses at each site.

After that we're planning to open a center at Central High School, and make that a hub for dental care. Opening up a dental care clinic in that high school would be a huge step and would provide a "double whammy" of service. Since Central High School has a vocational program to train the students as dental assistants, putting a dental clinic there would give a tremendous boost to that program. Those young men and women will be able to benefit from on-the-job training. The problem is that right now, the board of education is not putting any money into our program. In the special-needs school, for instance, we would need to construct a health center inside the school. The city of Newark has come through with some money, and we're hoping that the federal government can do something for us, too.

* * *

86

Caring For
All The Children

These school-based health care centers are a huge boon to the local community. The availability of health care to the children of Newark forms a huge step in improving the quality of life and opening the possibilities for the children of that city. The all-important safety net provided by access to regular health care will make a tremendous difference. Any young person falling inside the demographic within the city of Newark can simply walk into the school-based center and receive care.

By keeping their teeth healthy with our dental services, we will widen the possibilities of helping this young population avoid so many preventable health problems. We are trying to offer a total range of services to these children. Giving these young people access to pediatric, dental, and behavioral health care is one step toward offering them life-changing health care.

The Jewish Renaissance Medical Center gives every child a consent form for the parents. As long as we have a signed consent form on file, that student can receive any care he or she needs. If a student becomes ill during the course of the day, the staff in the health care center can evaluate and treat the child. We will be able to remove contagious children from the classroom and begin to address the illness, not just sidetrack it. If the child has an injury or any illness that could put the child at risk of more serious problems, the nurse practitioner can make the judgment to call the parent or send the child to the emergency room.

The health center staff can also arrange for specialty care with our other providers, such as a cardiologist or pulmonologist, if necessary. Most of the kids in each school are signed up for coverage in these centers, including dental care if necessary. Some of the centers offer more comprehensive care and are reaching out to cover more issues. Most of the children we treat in these school-based clinics are covered by Medicaid or charity care.

The Jewish Renaissance Medical Center is proud to be able to bring help and care to these children who, for the most part, would otherwise go without basic care. Our school-based health care system provides secondary benefits also. By taking care of children's health, we also help the family. Placing wellness visits and even emergency care in the schools purview allows parents, and especially single parents, to remain at work while the child receives medical care. The entire family benefits. Parents are always informed of the status of their child's health.

We are a really cohesive team. That's a crucial necessity for the smooth functioning of this large enterprise. Everyone works with a smile. We've got all the ingredients for success. I believe that we are one of the most progressive and innovative health care centers in the country. We utilize electronic medical records in all our health care centers and satellites. That means that patients from the Newark school-based centers, or ones treated by the medical/dental van, are part of the database. These patients' records can be accessed in a second from any one of our points of service.

It is a proven fact that a healthy child can learn more effectively. So by providing this comprehensive health care umbrella within the school system, we are playing a role in educating Newark's youth. I'm very proud and pleased that we can offer that kind of first-rate service.

* * *

87

Dreams Into Reality

SEARCHING FOR THE PERFECT BUILDING

*I*n the days when we were limited to serving Perth Amboy with our small four-room medical center, we were in fierce competition to meet the requirements for federal status. By stepping into the arena of the school-based medical centers, and taking over clinics at Raritan Bay Medical Center, we started on the road toward the expansion we knew we needed. The total number of patients we were able to treat at the little center in Perth Amboy, the school-based centers, and the hospital, permitted us to reach the numbers we needed to qualify. We were on our way toward the creation of the state-of-the-art medical center we finally opened in October 2008.

I was still in a quandary about the physical plant itself. The Perth Amboy health center was just too small. We needed a large main building;

we needed a real medical center. We started looking all over for a structure to serve our target population's needs.

Our search turned into a bigger challenge than we realized. We didn't have the resources to even begin a search like this. Our desires outstripped our monetary possibilities. What we wanted was nearly impossible at that point. We didn't have a cash reserve, and we didn't have the resources to support this project. We had no idea how we were going to pull this off. We located some buildings that would have served our purposes. We tried to instigate negotiations, but some of them didn't want to work with us. There were some nonprofits that owned buildings, but they didn't want to sell or didn't want to sell to us.

The building right across the street from our own little medical center on Hobart Street was up for sale. It was the old Sears Roebuck and Co. building from the 1950s. The owner wanted two million dollars for it. If I remember correctly, I had to come up with 10 percent for the purchase of that piece of real estate. We got part of the money through an earmark allocation, part through monies we raised, and then we dug into our own pockets. I put in a hundred thousand dollars of my own money, and Judy Goldberg put in another fifty thousand of her own. We really put our home equity to good use.

We finally hired George O'Shea, a businessman who specialized in developing business plans for this type of grant. He had formerly worked at the Department of Community Affairs for the state of New Jersey. He brought the necessary know-how into our game plan. We applied for and received two hundred thousand dollars from the New Jersey Redevelopment Authority. This was a fantastic opportunity. If our project ever collapsed, we wouldn't be on the hook. We wouldn't have to pay that money back. But, if the project went forward, we would have to pay it back. A pretty good deal for us at that moment.

The Economic Development Authority for the State of New Jersey gave us another fifty thousand dollars under much the same conditions. Now we had two hundred fifty thousand dollars. Between the grants, Judy's money, and mine, we actually had a total of four hundred thousand dollars. Putting down 10 percent or even 20 percent would not require more than we had.

We weren't there yet, though. The banks were having a hard time getting the entire proposal completed. George O'Shea wrote a business proposal amounting to about fourteen million dollars. This proposal included all the renovations, the equipment, and materials. This took us quite a while to work out. We had virtually no money to put this project on its feet. We were wracking our brains to find a way to move this along. At this point, we couldn't find a bank that would partner with us on this project.

Rob O'Neill, our project manager, was a high school friend of mine with whom I re-connected at our fortieth high school reunion. We were catching up at the reunion, and I was telling him all about this project. He had retired because he had leukemia. But he was itching to dig in to a project; he was eager to oversee the whole thing. I got him involved on the board. He loved it and jumped right in. He loved the idea of participating in a mission for providing health care to the underserved. He just took over the project and started looking at construction costs.

We ran into some problems, though. The cost went from five million dollars in 2003 to eight million in 2006, due to inflation (right at the beginning of construction). Steel had doubled in price. We were also actively searching for an architect. We interviewed quite a few until we finally selected one. The company we chose drew up the initial concept for the plans. I was very involved in this phase, too. I had a vision for this medical center. I wanted it to represent something more than a "medical" environment. What I envisioned was more of a "spa" experience. I wanted it to be open and inviting, a welcoming space. I wanted it to have a nice flow as well.

All my ideas were great, but the funding became a gigantic issue again. We started to run out of funding, and no one would pick up the cost of what we were planning. George O'Shea was bringing a lot of people to the table, but the project had hit a road block. One bank seemed interested, but, in general, the banks were hanging back. We didn't have enough invested in the building or even sufficient assets for any bank to lend us up to seven and a half million dollars. I considered fundraising events, or perhaps a sponsor.

Senator Menendez, who at that time was a congressman, was in town for an event we were running. We met in my office and discussed many things. High on the list was the plan for the medical center and the problems we were facing to move this project along. We discussed the feasibility of an earmark grant to add to the funding source for this building. He promised to try. The first year the earmark allocations came out, we received almost six hundred eighty thousand dollars. That did it for us. We were over the hump. Now we were in a position where the banks would speak to us. Then I got a letter from the mayor, the Honorable Joseph Vas. He promised us one million dollars from the Urban Enterprise Zone…grant money from the city to us. What a surprise that was. Although our project was becoming a bit more enticing to the banks, they were still not moving. Papers were lost, time was dragging, the project seemed to be going backward. It was very frustrating to me.

We forged ahead with this ambitious plan and bought the Sears Roebuck and Co. building in 2003. Part of the money for the down payment came from the earmark allocation that Senator Menendez helped us achieve. We know that earmarks are a hot-potato topic today, but if it weren't for Senator Menendez's help in securing the earmark, we would never have been able to build the medical center. In this case, we didn't build a road to nowhere, we built a health care center that provides quality health care for the uninsured and the working poor. We were trying hard to do this on our own, but the banks wouldn't work with us. We had no collateral to qualify for a mortgage. At that time there were no federal funds available to build or renovate Federally Qualified Health Centers.

We were in and out of bank offices. I went to Provident Bank right here in Perth Amboy. Chris Martin, the president of the bank, said this type of project was a perfect fit for them. This was a community-building effort. We talked about the benefits for Perth Amboy and the surrounding areas. He really wanted to help us do this. So his bank gave us a "letter of commitment" for seven and a half million dollars of funding. We were on the move.

Unfortunately, right after we dug in, and the project was under way, Rob O'Neill fell ill again and passed away. I was devastated; he was a very close longtime friend, as well as an ally on this project. I would sorely miss this wonderful friend. Not only was this heartbreaking, but we were without a project manager. We needed someone who knew what was going on, who knew the day-to-day needs of the project, and who would oversee it. The "shoe man" just couldn't do it himself. I went to the board, and one of the board members suggested Robert Karabinchack. So we had our new project manager.

The outside of the former Sears Roebuck and Co. building was in good shape. But we needed to gut the entire structure—all forty-eight thousand square feet—so we could design it the right way. We wanted it to suit our future clients' medical needs perfectly. Often, when buildings are used or built to serve the uninsured or the lower economic groups, no care is given to design. Typically, decrepit old buildings are simply re-purposed, and no thought is given to what they look like. I didn't want to overlook the design. I wanted our medical center to be beautiful. I envisioned glass and stucco. It wasn't easy, and the oversight was tremendous. We really needed to stay on the ball and keep check on the contractors. We were supposed to be done in twelve months, but it went to eighteen. At least we did it.

We needed to work hard to get the best rates on the money. The most sensible way was to bond. The Economic Development Authority (EDA) was going to bond seven and a half million dollars for us. Provident was going to buy it back. Now our rate was down to a manageable 4 percent. In our proposal, EDA was going to loan us two million dollars at 3 percent. We now had the money to begin the conversion of that building. We started construction at the beginning of 2006. From start to finish, the building conversion took us eighteen months. We walked into the building in October 2008. All told, we got one and a half million dollars through the efforts of Senator Menendez. The grand opening ceremony was a monumental moment.

* * *

88

Establishing The Model For Health Care

Before we even started construction on the medical center, we had a proposal for transferring all the primary care clinics from the Raritan Bay Medical Center to the Jewish Renaissance Medical Center around 2005. That hospital was losing money and having trouble keeping its doors open for charity-care patients. The proposal included the offer for us to use one of their buildings right there on their campus. This was only until our new medical center was completed. They weren't charging us rent, which proved to be a tremendous aid to us. It was an interesting offer, because we were so small at that time. Using the physical plant at Raritan Bay Medical Center gave us enlarged possibilities. We could set up an entire floor to serve our pediatrics unit, and on another level establish internal medicine and obstetrics care. Now we had a physical layout that expanded the potential of our medical care.

Raritan Bay closed down all their primary care clinics, and we stepped in and took them over. The Raritan Bay Medical Center residency program still utilized the lower floors in the afternoons. That also served our needs and our patients in a strong way. We had just expanded and didn't have to lay out the cost of a new building or equipment. We could continue to serve the public until our new building construction was complete.

When the brand new medical center was finally complete, we were able to consolidate all of our medical services. We merged the two sites—the one on the campus of the Raritan Bay Medical Center, and the little center we had been operating on Hobart Street. This was a huge move and a huge moment.

At the beginning, we were actively searching for personnel to meet the expanding needs of the medical center, but it was difficult. Our organization grew in fits and starts. The search for the right individual for each role wasn't a simple challenge either. Some of the people who came onboard at first were here for the money. I think we had five medical directors before finding the person who really served the medical center's needs. I took some flak because we seemed to be running through directors for a while. But I countered that criticism with the fact that I needed to put the medical center, our programs, and the clients we serve, first. I would not keep an employee if I was not satisfied with that person's performance.

The coordination of personnel, records, and all the little details that were required to fall into place to allow us to serve the public were myriad and specialized. We had to assure that everyone was up to speed on everything and felt that we needed to handle this rigorously and scrupulously. So we held a retreat to carry out that part of the plan. By gathering everyone away from other distractions, we were able to handle and cover more than we could with a series of meetings or other communications methods. We needed to be sure that everyone involved was as up to date as possible on the Electronic Medical Records (EMR) system we were installing. We started using the EMR in August 2008 in preparation for the definitive move into the new Medical Arts Center in October.

What we have established in Perth Amboy will serve as a model for health care centers throughout our country. The Raritan Bay Medical Center is still open, handling other facets of a rounded-out complete health care service for the local population, mostly specialty care. What we have running in tandem with the Raritan Bay Medical Center is working so well that other locales have asked us to participate with them. So many of these hospitals' caseloads consist of charity-care or Medicaid patients. Our medical center is geared specifically to offer primary and dental care to the underserved populations. The problem is always a financial one. All of these Federally Qualified Health Centers receive funding from the same State of New Jersey charity-care pool. The total amount of available funds is large, but it is finite. The state begins its fiscal year in July, and we had already maxed out our charity-care funds by January. There is a cap on the amount each center can use from its charity-care pool. Surpassing that cap amounts to providing health care without reimbursement. No center can afford that.

So, the Jewish Renaissance Medical Center has entered into discussions with hospitals in other townships to study the feasibility of our collaborating with them. We studied this option with a hospital in a northern New Jersey town that serves a large uninsured population, after they approached us. We calculated that we would require a grant from them of at least two million dollars. We estimated that amount based on the fact that we would be seeing around twenty thousand charity care-patient visits, and that would equal the reimbursement that we would receive from the New Jersey State charity-care pool. It would save the hospital much more money, plus we would be paying for the staff, rent, and other day-to-day running expenses. This collaboration never got off the ground, because our charity-care pool was maxed out, and they didn't want to grant us the two million dollars to see these charity-care patients. In effect, it would have saved them over five million dollars.

We will be meeting with another south New Jersey hospital to discuss a possible collaboration with them. The reality is, we will only be able to work with them if they grant us the money for their charity-care patients.

We are all attempting to accomplish what any national or governmental health care reform would attempt. We want to provide the neediest with comprehensive preventive and quality health care.

We receive monies for each patient we see. We get a hundred and one dollars for every charity-care patient, and around one hundred thirty-seven dollars for each Medicaid patient. That is what the Jewish Renaissance Medical Center receives for an encounter…for everything that we provide for a patient. The Jewish Renaissance Medical Center makes sure that everyone sees a doctor whether he or she can afford it or not. We simply believe that access to medical care is a crucial human requirement.

* * *

89

The Robert Menendez
Medical Arts Center

The support of Senator Robert Menendez was crucial in the process of creating the Jewish Renaissance Medical Center. If it weren't for his support and diligence in helping to secure the designation of a Federally Qualified Health Center, and for aiding with the funding for renovation of our new state-of-the-art medical center, we might never have achieved it. The day our medical center opened, as I cut the ribbon, I couldn't help but picture so many of the moments, the hard work, the growing team of purpose-driven people who had worked so hard, our boards of directors, our donors, our politicians…the list is huge. An undertaking like this doesn't happen without a surge of passion from so many fronts. It also doesn't happen without heart.

I love looking at the building itself. It's a testament to the heart I inherited from the Paleys and the Goldsmiths, who demonstrated with their every action that giving and sharing is as important as anything else that makes a person's life worthwhile. Here is tangible proof of the power of that nickel Grandpa Hymie asked me to drop into that man's cup on that long-ago Friday afternoon. Here is proof of that power...multiplied a million-fold. Here is that shiny nickel represented anew in this gleaming building. The medically underserved population of Middlesex County now has a destination.

The ribbon-cutting ceremony opening the Robert Menendez Medical Arts Center on Hobart Street, Perth Amboy, NJ., October 27, 2008. Left to right: Mark Roberts (CEO of Med. Ctr.); Hon. Wilda Diaz, Mayor; Sen. Robert Menendez; Judy Goldberg (CEO of JRF); and Dr. Alan Goldsmith, founder.

With the opening of this strictly outpatient center, we are equipped to offer total care to the families and individuals who would otherwise not receive comprehensive medical care. The center's care covers pediatric, ob-gyn, internal medicine, and dental care disciplines. The fact that we renovated this medical center from the first stone to the last meant that we could better control the utilization of space.

We created a horseshoe-shaped configuration on the first floor to allow for a natural flow of a large number of patient exam rooms. We wanted this floor to be pleasing to the eye and well designed for its purpose, too.

At the beginning, the first floor was designed to hold all three core disciplines. I had a feeling that it would not be sufficient for the growing population we needed to serve. I'm really glad I took that long, critical look at the plans. We had a medically suitable space that we were originally planning to lease out. Instead of allowing that, I confiscated the space of about thirty-five hundred feet and created a Women's Wellness Center with nine exam rooms. That meant that pediatrics was established on the first floor with nine exam rooms, and internal medicine with another ten exam rooms.

Setting up a section for dental care was another story altogether. The University of Dentistry of New Jersey designed something for me. One of my board members, from Eastern Dental, had already given me about seventeen centers around New Jersey to handle dental care under the Operation U.S.A. model. He had taken a look at what we were trying to do in our brand new medical center and said it wasn't viable. He asked me to let his people handle this aspect of the center. They came up with a feasible and workable model. His team designed eleven dental operatories for the medical center. Eight were designed as bays and three as quiet rooms. It's working out fantastically. It's a good thing we followed his lead; the dental wing is working to capacity, and the demand is huge.

I continued to make changes to the original plan as we built the center. Originally I thought we could make good use of the board room. On paper it looked big, but I soon realized we couldn't fit our one hundred twenty employees in that space. So I took more of the space that had been set aside for leasing, and turned it into a Community Room. We wanted this center to belong to the community, and this space brought us a step closer to this goal. Anyone in the community can access this space. The people of Perth Amboy can use this room for meetings or gatherings. Plus, we achieve full use of the space by holding staff meetings there, training sessions, or whatever else presents itself.

This new center is a modern, totally up-to-date structure. We are energy conscious. For instance, lights go on and off automatically in response to people entering and leaving rooms. We have built a totally "green" building. Another one of the fantastic innovations we have is an isolation room with a HEPA filtering system. It's near the intake and reception area. If a person arrives at the center and the staff fears that this individual carries anthrax, smallpox, or any other infectious disease, they can put him or her in this room to prevent spreading the disease or pathogen. A doctor or nurse will see the patient right in that isolated, filtered environment.

We wanted this medical center to establish an enviable level of care for our patients. On the ground floor, upon entering the center, a visitor sees the receptionist. An incoming patient goes there, where the individual is guided to the registration area. From registration, the patient is sent to the section for specialty care he or she needs, such as pediatrics, ob-gyn, internal medicine, or dental. That patient registers with the unit clerk, and waits until he or she is called into the exam room to see the physician. The unit clerk also receives all the calls for that department. That whole process of registering and seeing a physician should take about a half hour.

We do a complete background intake on the patient's address, income, and family history. This information helps us make a determination about the type of care necessary and the source of funding for this person's care. This helps us determine whether a particular patient is eligible for Medicaid or will become a charity-care patient. The patient can also receive care on his or her own insurance or simply pay for the care. The self-paying patients are billed on a sliding scale according to family income. For example, a person with four children earning about twenty thousand a year would be eligible for charity care. Most children in New Jersey automatically qualify for Medicaid because the laws are written that way. The children are given that protection. If a patient has visited before, the process is much shorter.

The entire medical system that we run in New Jersey is connected via electronic medical records. Patient records are created, stored, and retrieved electronically. We worked hard to make this data system a reality, and our doctors are now able to access any information on a patient from any of our centers. That means the medical/dental vans, the school-based medical centers, and the Jewish Renaissance Medical Center are all linked.

We've had the system for over a year, and like all software, it requires fine-tuning and upkeep. But it simplifies and hones our ability to service our patients. We can avoid repeating tests, which is a great time and money saving benefit. All new doctors have to be trained on the system.

Another fantastic benefit involves easy access. Let's say a patient phones the on-call doctor at night. Even if this doctor has no personal knowledge of this patient, the doctor can access the patient's medical records right on his or her home computer, or PDA, and give the patient advice based on the information gathered.

We constructed a pharmacy on the first floor of the medical center. We're going to lease the space to a Perth Amboy pharmacy. Having it right there in the building will simplify things, too. It will offer convenience and efficiency for our doctors and patients. The pharmacy will run our 340 B program for pharmaceuticals. This is a federal program for Federally Qualified Health Centers and hospitals. Anyone who qualifies for this program will receive anywhere from a 20 to 40 percent discount off the price of the medicine. Also, if the prescription is written in one of our dental or medical centers, it can be sent directly to the pharmacy's computer via our EMR system.

Patients do pay for their own prescriptions, but with that generous discount. If a patient can't afford to pay even the discounted amount for medicine, our intake people can help them apply to the pharmaceutical companies for help. Some of these companies will donate medications. Our intake people help them fill out the forms, and we forward them to the companies. The meds then come directly to our center, and we dispense them to the patient. All of this means that seniors, charity-care patients, and so many others who have not previously been cared for will be served.

* * *

90

Equestrian Camps For Special-Needs Children

For the next eight chapters, I want to enumerate and discuss the Jewish Renaissance Foundation's involvement in other types of very special programs. The first one is very near and dear to my heart. Soon after we initiated our medical and overseas programs, I became aware of the need for a summer program to meet the requirements of special-needs children. The benefits to all children from organized and structured vacation camps are obvious to all. However, it is often the children who have developmental problems or other issues that preclude them from participating in some camp situations. We have found a marvelous way to set up a program to give children with special needs something edifying, instructional, and safe to fill their time. The Equestrian Camp was one of those great achievements for the Jewish Renaissance Foundation. We initiated this with a small grant from the Foundation.

I had been stymied for a while searching for a way to help children with special needs. These are children with Down syndrome and others with an array of developmental difficulties.

It's been known for years that animals have the ability to make strong healing connections with all people. For example, there are programs where dogs are taken to nursing homes or hospitals on a regular schedule, where the patients can touch them and spend time interacting. The benefit to the patients is well documented.

We designed a program for children who can't enjoy a regular camp experience due to their developmental issues. We called the program *Yaakov Yadayim*, or "Jacob's Hand." The program gave these children a safe place to have ample time to interact with animals and develop caring habits and ties to these "pets." This program occurred on my friend's horse farm in Monroe. The property was replete with chickens, horses, and ample room and time for picnics and all the monitored activities that could develop on a site like this.

Initially, we started this as a two-week camp program. The children learned to care for, bond with, and ride horses. Some of the kids were small, so we acquired a stand to allow them to mount up. The children were so animated; this was a new world for them, one that opened their experiences and confidence. Many parents shared stories of their children's excitement with me. They told me that they couldn't even tell the youngsters that they were heading to camp the next day, because their excitement would keep them up all night.

Most of the children who have participated in "Jacob's Hand" have never had any previous experience with horses. There were children at this camp who wouldn't even get close to one of these large animals. Yet, at the end of their two-week stay, they were riding. It was quite remarkable for all of us to witness the changes in these kids, to see how they had grown from this exposure and experience.

"Yaakov Yadayim" (Jacob's Hand) the Jewish Renaissance Foundation's Equestrian Camp for special needs children, summer, 1998.

Unfortunately, the funds weren't available the following year, so the camp didn't open that second year. After seeing the huge impact it had on these special-needs children, it goes without saying that the benefits are very important. I'd like to see this camp happen again, and on an ongoing basis.

* * *

267

91

Hydroponic Farming

HELPING YOUNG ADULTS WITH CHALLENGES

We have another project in the pipeline for young people. Someone will be donating nine acres of land to us. We're planning on capping this land with concrete slabs and installing hydroponic pods on them. This land is not suitable for traditional farming and planting, so we're planning on doing what has been accomplished on a large scale in Israel with hydroponic farming. With the pods in place, an organic vegetable farm will be planted. The whole operation will be connected by walkways. If you've ever seen a hydroponic farm, you know that the whole process is much cleaner and easier to work and maintain than traditional dirt farming.

The plan is for handicapped and mentally challenged young adults to be trained in the hydroponic farming process. This is a viable and sustainable activity that will give them skills, an income, and a trade. They will be involved in a process that sustains mankind by providing food, but also sustains those carrying out the tasks of caring for the farm, with a sense of connection to nature and the cycle of growth. These young men and women will have the ability to establish themselves as self-sufficient members of society. They'll be earning their own salaries.

Since we have nine acres, we can provide training and activities for quite a large number of young adults. We'll be approaching Public Service Electric and Gas for their help in installing solar power to run this operation. This will make us quite a "green" undertaking. We won't use any contaminating energy sources for pumping the water, heating the greenhouses, or ventilation. We are asking the Rutgers Agricultural School to take part in this project. Their involvement will provide invaluable insight for the participants, as well as scientific knowledge. The Rotary Club has also approached me about contributing to this endeavor. We know they will form an important partnership with us on this project.

I love this program for the opportunities it gives to these young people who are faced with life-altering problems. This hydroponic project and the training it will offer will help them begin to have a broader perspective on life. Since their parents can accompany them to the farm, this also becomes a moment for growing and experiencing new horizons together. Organic vegetables sell for a lot more than traditionally farmed produce. We plan to market and sell to local stores. We're hoping to offer pricing a bit below the normally higher ones. While at a fundraiser for one of Emeril Lagasse's charities, I met a wholesaler from New York who agreed to sell our produce. We are exploring the avenues to make this dream a reality and are looking forward to bringing this to light in the coming year.

* * *

92

Youthbuild Program

*T*he YouthBuild Program is another one that gives me a huge amount of satisfaction. This is a federal program under the aegis of the Department of Labor. And, we run it as part of the Jewish Renaissance Foundation. This allows us to reach out in a distinctive and proactive manner to older kids, and young men and women who have dropped out of high school. These people are often the ones who fall through the cracks and really get lost. When this cohort drops out of high school, they severely limit themselves to lives on the margins of society. As they get older, the desire, probability, and possibility of completing a GED, for example, lessens. Even if they were to complete the credits to earn a GED, where would they go from there? In their late teens, maybe early twenties, with a GED and no post-high school education or vocational training, they would still be virtually unemployable. Add to that the state of today's economy, and these kids would be headed nowhere.

Through our YouthBuild Program, young men and women who have dropped out of high school are given a second chance. We get them back into school and help them achieve the credits to earn their GED. The exceptional part of this program is that we offer them on-the-job, on-site, vocational training in the building trades.

A very big grant was the engine that made this great program possible, and is providing the impetus to keep it moving ahead. The Jewish Renaissance Foundation has established our own construction company as a part of this innovative program. I have found a very well-known and accomplished builder who is actually working with us. He looks at homes (maybe foreclosures, or abandoned real estate) and estimates the cost for rehabbing each structure and creating a habitable dwelling. We've also hired a chief supervisor who has been in the building business and who knows this industry very well. We plan to bring in another carpenter, too. Completing the team with our students, we have a viable construction company.

Teaching the kids as they work on the projects gives them the hands-on, skill-building construction savvy and practice to turn them into a valuable workforce asset. They complete their high school experience and learn a skilled trade. Throughout history the skilled trades have relied upon the apprentice experience; we've just built on that successful model and ended up with our own modern apprentices. Not only are they being trained by masters, but they're earning a high school diploma and getting paid at the same time. Because we don't have to pay outside people, which would be much more expensive, we can control costs. So we can rehab these homes for less money than a traditional company, and offer them lower prices, all while training the next generation of carpenters, plumbers, and general contractors.

* * *

93

The Community Action Agency

*T*he scope of the Jewish Renaissance Foundation is expanding all the time. In October 2009 we were designated a Community Action Agency. That means the federal government is giving the Foundation funding. In 2010, for our first and second year budgets, we received about $1.8 million. One of the areas into which we are placing that money is in our Workforce Investment Program; another is in low-cost housing. We have developed these programs ourselves and are instituting them in Middlesex County, New Jersey.

In addition, the city of Perth Amboy has received a grant from the Department of Community Affairs of the State of New Jersey for the Neighborhood Stabilization Program. Once the city received that grant, and we became the sub-recipient of $1.7 million through Perth Amboy's Department of Community Affairs, this gave us the ability to rehabilitate foreclosed or abandoned housing. We will be in a strong position to do a lot more good for people caught in the recent economic downslide.

Through the Community Action Agency we are funding the Academy for Workforce Investment. We have the capacity to help men and women caught in the downward spiral of the job market through this channel. We design programs where we see need, and we are always searching for ways to help our community. For example, we distribute food vouchers to families on various holidays throughout the year to help those who have lost jobs, suffer from illness, or find themselves burdened by other factors that impact wages and well-being. We can offer retraining to men and women to help them get back into the job market and on their feet again. Also, we are preparing to help low-income families acquire their own homes.

In 2009 we involved ourselves in Client Assistance Funds, a way to help people who found themselves in difficult financial moments. Since the implosion of the economy, we have all seen and read about the tremendous problems for individuals and families who have fallen on very hard times. Often they can't keep up with their mortgage payments, have trouble paying a heating bill, or can't make one or more rent payments. We offer help to people who have fallen into these situations with a one-time arrangement so they won't lose their homes, have to survive the winter without heat, or be evicted for non-payment of rent. They can use this aid for food or any other immediate need. To qualify for help under the auspices of the Community Action Agency, the applicants need to be 125 percent under the poverty level. For example, a family of four earning around $40,000, or a family of five bringing in $50,000 a year would be eligible for this type of help.

THE COMMUNITY DEVELOPMENT CORPORATION (CDC)

I saw a very big need for low-cost housing all around us in Perth Amboy. Every day we were hearing about people losing jobs and falling into a spiral of hopelessness. Every day the local news was full of these human interest stories. We established, with a separate board of directors, the Jewish Renaissance Community Development Corporation. I wanted to set up something that was a separate entity, but would be under the umbrella of the Jewish Renaissance Foundation for liability purposes. When you're dealing with construction and rehab work, this is a big consideration.

Under the Community Development Corporation, funding will be available through the Community Development Block Grant Program for help in the acquisition and rehabilitation of these homes. As a nonprofit, it means we can now do any of the rehabilitation of foreclosed homes or construction of low-cost housing throughout the entire state.

NEIGHBORHOOD STABILIZATION PROGRAM

The Neighborhood Stabilization Program stands on its own with respect to grant monies. It's a one-time program. According to the grant the Jewish Renaissance Foundation wrote, the city is the lead agency and we are the sub-grantee for $1.7 million from the state of New Jersey to begin the Neighborhood Stabilization Program right here in Perth Amboy. This is a huge and important program any time, but during this recession, even more so. Many homes were being abandoned by families unable to pay mortgages. In many cases, the houses were trashed or just left in disrepair until they became more and more rundown. The effect of all of this was devastating to home values, quality of life, viability of neighborhoods, and to the other people struggling to maintain their loans and stay in their homes.

We now had the ability to take foreclosed and abandoned homes, put money and time into rehabilitating them, and sell them below value by using grant money. We would also be training young people through our YouthBuild Program. One benefit is our ability to maintain lower construction costs, but it is not the only benefit of this initiative. Borrowed from history, we bring the apprentice system to life in our town to give these twenty-first-century young men and women a real chance to succeed; the instruction and on-the-job training will lead them into lifelong professions. Teaching a trade to our young people and ending up with fully refurbished, habitable and lower-costing homes at the same time is a win-win.

However, the recession has presented us with some unique and perplexing problems in carrying out this plan. The grants (for acquisition of houses) place limits on their use, and these rules can create problems for us. For example, one of the regulations states that we can only buy a house at 1 percent below the appraisal value. Let's say a bank is holding a property in which they have two hundred thousand dollars invested. Maybe we would offer them one hundred seventy thousand or one hundred eighty thousand. But in today's market, the appraisal comes in low, let's say at one hundred forty-five thousand. We can't offer the amount we'd like and feel it is a fair offer; we are bound by the rules of the grant to offer 1 percent below that lower appraised price. So we have to rescind our original bid and offer less than the appraised value. The banks won't accept that low bid, and we can't purchase the house. This isn't just happening to us here, but all around the country. So we find ourselves almost eight months into the grant, and we're still having some difficulty acquiring homes because of that "glitch."

BUILDING COMMUNITIES, INC.
(A NONPROFIT CORPORATION)

The Neighborhood Stabilization Program is the avenue leading to the Building Communities Corporation (an offshoot of the Jewish Renaissance Foundation) where they can do the actual construction and train the young people. It also helps that we're able to generate a small profit from this construction company. This profit goes right back into the process and allows us to create more affordable housing for more people.

There are guidelines controlling who can apply for one of these homes. Through our Neighborhood Stabilization Program, we locate these families with a public lottery. We advertise in papers and through fliers. Anyone can enter. From the hundreds of names sent to us, we pick out three groups of forty each. Starting with the first one, we send each family to our financial counselors who are Housing and Urban Development (HUD) certified. They study each case separately to see if the family qualifies for a mortgage. If they don't qualify, we can't sell them a house. We do work with each family to try to help them qualify. These people may have suffered a bankruptcy, or they may just owe a lot of money. Our financial counselors try to help them set up a workable program with attainable goals. If they can clean up their financial record, maybe down the line we can help them purchase a house. In the meantime, we can help them rent. Once we have determined who qualifies for a mortgage, we present the houses that are available for them.

The participants in the Neighborhood Stabilization Program need to look at a house that would qualify their income status for a mortgage. For this group, we might put one hundred eight thousand dollars into a project and sell it for one hundred fifty thousand. The importance of the grant money becomes very evident here. We use the grant monies to make up the difference.

* * *

94

The Twenty-First-Century Community Learning Centers Program

The Jewish Renaissance Foundation is also active in this initiative as a sponsor of an after school program. We have received a $2.5 million grant over five years to make this a reality. School-aged children are offered after-school tutoring, enrichment of various types, music classes, salsa class, and educational trips through this school-based service. It's another way to keep our children safe while providing fun and interesting experiences for them. It gives us an opportunity to enrich our town by enriching our children; our children are our future.

* * *

95

The Boys & Girls Club Of Perth Amboy—2006

T he Boys & Girls Clubs of America has a long and very distinguished past. Generations of people have experienced for themselves, or know of others who have benefited from their work with children. The Boys & Girls Clubs have contributed solid values and support for children in need of a place to spend their free time, and have been fundamental in helping them grow up the right way. As with so many of the programs and areas in which we work today, I look for a need and then try to create a way to fix it, give help, and share with those in need. We saw in this organization another means to keep children safe when they were not in school or at home.

It often seems as if some terrible event has to occur to spark an idea that could have prevented the incident in the first place. It was like that for the impetus to start a Boys & Girls Club in our city. In this instance it was a tragedy that occurred in Perth Amboy's Willow Park Pond around the time our medical center was under construction. That particular summer, unsupervised kids roamed the town with nothing to do. They decided to play in and around the pond. One of them got into trouble there and drowned. The town was really rocked by this news. And I knew that there was a way to prevent its happening again. We needed a cost-effective way to offer the children a place where they could spend after-school time safely.

Yvonne Lopez, a former Jewish Renaissance Foundation board member, and I were compelled to start a Boys & Girls Club. We saw the creation of this entity in Perth Amboy as a way to create and sustain a place where free time for kids would be productive, safe, and supervised. We wanted to harness the power that these clubs have always had for the benefit of the children's lives in our own city.

It wasn't an easy task to get this undertaking started. We needed to enlist the help of the Foundation that oversees the entire Boys & Girls Clubs system. We needed to secure funding—a huge task in itself. Then we had to find a physical place to hold the group. There was a possibility of running the Boys & Girls Clubs in the schools, but there were criteria that needed to be met in order to establish the group in that venue.

The Boys & Girls Clubs of America had a problem with the Foundation overseeing the whole shebang, so that didn't work out. This was the first venture of its kind. Due to the fact the Jewish Renaissance Foundation was proposing the funding, we needed to oversee the whole thing. I went to the organization and explained to them why this needed to occur and how we could structure it. We put together a model that they accepted. The Boys & Girls Clubs board of trustees would vote on resolutions and would pass their decisions on to the Foundation's board of directors for the final vote. It turned out they liked the idea, so we were able to get this fantastic project off the ground in 2006.

The Foundation was overseeing its operations and was helping with funding. The reports came to our board of directors at the Foundation, and we acted on them. We have helped Boys & Girls Clubs of America see how this new model could be used to open up more of these great clubs for children. We're now in three schools in Perth Amboy serving over seven hundred children with after-school programs and summer camp programs. We are also in Carteret High School serving approximately four hundred fifty more children.

We help the Boys & Girls Clubs in other ways, too. If they need help with payroll, we loan them money. That was our concept all along. Under the wing of the Foundation, the clubs had a better chance of succeeding and completing this task for the children of our town. No child is ever turned away.

* * *

96

Yvonne Lopez's Comments (2010)

We started up the Boys & Girls Club. It was always a dream of mine and a vision of Alan's. I chair that board. We've been operating under the auspices of the Jewish Renaissance Foundation for the last four years. If it were not for the Jewish Renaissance Foundation, I'm not sure the Boys & Girls Club would have been established in Perth Amboy.

The formation of the Boys & Girls Club was propelled by two separate incidents, tragic incidents. One was a drowning, and the other involved the suffocation of three kids from Camden. The week before the drowning, three little kids were playing in eighty-five-degree heat in abandoned cars in a lot. They went into the trunk of a car, and they locked themselves in. They suffocated to death. That shows what propelled us. And after that we had a youth drown.

I called Alan; we were both in tears. We had to do something; we had to keep our kids off the streets. The Boys & Girls Club provides a place for kids to be after school and in the summer.

Recently we faced a massive funding cutback. We lost two hundred fifty thousand dollars. We started an aggressive fundraising campaign, and we're going to stay open. We will have our summer camp. The donations are coming in.

You know, thirty employees volunteered to work without pay for the month of March. All are part-timers, all teachers. They come after school. And they said they will work without pay while we restructure the budget program. They love this program that much.

* * *

97

A Mother's Words

(AT A BOYS & GIRLS CLUB RECEPTION ON MAY 13, 2010)

*G*ood evening. I'm so proud to be here speaking to you tonight. I want to tell you what The Boys & Girls Club means to me and my children. I've lived in Perth Amboy my entire life and did not have the opportunities that my kids have. We didn't have activities or groups that met after school.

I got pregnant at sixteen. Now I'm in my thirties, and I have three children. I'm a single mother, and it's not easy for me. I have to work.

The Boys & Girls Club in our town gives my three kids a safe and structured place to be after school. I can be at work and not worry. I know where my children are, who they are with, and what they are doing. And I know they're doing good things. They come home every day with their homework finished. They are with adults who supervise and guide them. They are involved in interesting and fun *activities. I can work for our family without worrying that they will get into trouble. And I know that the wonderful people at the Boys & Girls Club will give them good activities. They can avoid the mistakes I made.*

I just wanted you all to know how grateful I am to have the Boys & Girls Club in Perth Amboy. My family offers a good example of how these people help our children.

* * *

98

The Future

There is a saying by Rashi, the Jewish sage, "We're all one people, one heart." That's the way I feel. We're all different heights, skin colors, hair colors, weights, but there's a reason behind it all. G-d made us all different on the outside, but the same on the inside. It's our job, our life's work, to try to come together and make our civilization better. That's my goal; that's the goal of the Jewish Renaissance Family of Organizations. That's what we're all doing here. We believe that so strongly that we have borrowed Rashi's wise words to create our Foundation's credo, "One People, One Heart."

The members of all the boards of directors are already telling me, "We want you around for a hundred twenty years. You're the catalyst to all the organizations and all the boards. What'll happen if you're not here? What will be your legacy?"

First of all, as long as we have a strong foundation and base for our organizations, I know our work will continue. I believe every person is replaceable, including me. I don't see a problem. I see myself only as a humble man who is carrying out the will of the Almighty and the model set by my ancestors. The Jewish Renaissance Family of Organizations is a growing entity held together by people who all share the same vision about helping others. Hopefully, my legacy and this vision are being burnt and chiseled into the very stones of our Foundation. Hopefully, with or without me, the wonderful and dedicated staff and board members of the Jewish Renaissance Family of Organizations will continue to move forward with one goal in mind...to help their fellow men and women.

What I can do now, and what I am doing, is creating an environment of cooperation and sharing. By bringing together all the CEOs from all the organizations on a regular basis, we all stay connected and informed. We meet every week so that each organization knows what the others are doing. We are able to collaborate to ensure that all our programs are best serving our clientele. The scope of the work of the various programs within the Jewish Renaissance Family of Organizations is, therefore, not foreign to those not directly involved, but communicated, so that there is an overall direction in which the Jewish Renaissance Family of Organizations moves now and continues to move.

I also intermingle people on the various boards. That way, for instance, a board member for the Jewish Renaissance Foundation is also on the medical center board. We need to maintain a flow of information, ideas, and plans. It's the perfect way for the Jewish Renaissance Family of Organizations to remain a vital, growing entity. Information travels among the boards and the board members; everyone knows what everyone else is doing. We can maintain our focus, prevent ourselves from "getting stale," and maintain the immediacy and vibrancy of the Jewish Renaissance Family of Organizations.

As far as the future of the Jewish Renaissance Family of Organizations, we're going to develop a centralized fundraising department. That way all our organizations can come under one fundraising and gathering umbrella so that we're not repeatedly asking the same people, or the same agencies, for funds. We can coordinate our fundraising into one area and split the donations between our organizations. Up until now, we have been 90 percent funded by grants, and we have to change that.

I'd like to see us undertake more international medical missions. But we are so busy that one person can't service it all. Eventually I'm going to have someone take over the role of supervising the overseas missions. I can't be deploying myself overseas continuously while staying on top of what's going on here, too.

As I mentioned, the lifespan of start-up nonprofits usually runs from one to seven years. The Jewish Renaissance Foundation is moving into its fifteenth year. It seems like a dream; we've undergone such phenomenal growth in this decade and a half. From the back of the shoe store, to distant shores, we've made great changes in the lives of so many people around New Jersey and throughout the world.

* * *

99

Tom Devlin's Comments

*A*lan and I have stayed in touch all these years. Over the many years, we've corresponded and talked. Since my wife went to college with Alan and me, she knows him extremely well. We were talking about how proud we are of him, of what he's done with his life. From working in the Peace Corps, then going home to Jersey to teach and coach in Perth Amboy, then taking over his father's shoe store. He saw the need of people all around him, and it put him on a path to help them.

What Alan is doing is touching humanity. He has extended himself and his family in such a way as to help so many people. He makes everybody feel good. And it is big.

I joke with him about retiring. I said recently, "How long are you going to do this? I'm enjoying the heck out of retirement…playing golf, enjoying my boat…" But he just loves what he's doing. He loves the people. Alan is the most "people *person" you'll ever meet. I've been blessed in my life to know a lot of good people. I would have to rank Alan's efforts on behalf of his Foundation as magnificent. He's doing everything we wish we could do to help people. What else can I say? I absolutely admire it.*

What he has done is so large and so unique. It taps the talents of so many people. That's what a good administrator does. He knows what his mission is, surrounds himself with good people, and allows those people to "do their thing." I don't think he's the type of person who tries to tell people how to use their strengths, but simply allows them to use those strengths in the most productive ways.

* * *

100

Re-Evaluating A Life

*T*hinking back to the beginnings of the Jewish Renaissance Foundation, I am reminded how I strove to make each and every step sustainable…from funding, to providing social services , dental and medical care to the most needful populations. That was a very important part of my goal. It was of primary importance to me that the Jewish Renaissance Foundation with all its branches, was a sustainable model.

Moving in that direction not only involved opening up the funding options, but also establishing competent and motivated boards of directors. Looking around at the highly educated, dedicated, motivated, and extremely intelligent women and men who occupy positions on the various boards of the Jewish Renaissance Family of Organizations, I am content. Although I am the "face" of the Jewish Renaissance Family of Organizations, it no longer is "mine" alone. So many people are invested in the work we are doing. So many people are giving so much of their time and their hearts. Truly we are doing the Almighty's work.

No entity should depend on one person alone. That is selfish, foolish, and wrong. The most important basic reason for the fallibility of a model based on one person is the fact that we're all mortal. The continuance and the wonderful work of the Jewish Renaissance Family of Organizations should not balance on my shoulders alone. And now it doesn't. That's just the way it's supposed to be.

That's especially important, because the need for our services is growing. I myself grow older each year, and the Jewish Renaissance Family of Organizations must continue its mission. Further, about six years ago, I came face to face again with my own mortality. And, once again, found that G-d's plans for me were not complete.

* * *

101

A Personal Challenge

*I*n April of 2003, I was forced to take another good look at myself.
My doctors told me that my PSA test (prostate-specific antigens)
was elevated. They gave me a high dose of antibiotics. The next year
the PSA was higher. The docs sent me for an MRI, but saw nothing. More
antibiotics did little to lower those alarming numbers. So, after a biopsy,
we found out the worst. About 20 percent of my prostate was cancerous.
The options were laid out for me, and luckily today's medicine offers us
various roads to take. But I knew what I wanted, and that was to get rid of
that killer.

I chose to have it all removed. At that time, the CyberKnife option was
not available, so I really had to "go under the knife." That was quite a shock
for me. Here I was at fifty-six years old never having had an operation, and
now I was faced with the dreaded big "C," and my first operation.

I felt comfortable the night before the surgery, but still a bit concerned and nervous. Whatever "sins" I had committed in my life, whatever bad I might have done, I felt hopeful that the good I had done would count in a big way. At least I hoped so. My wife, sister, and I went to dinner and a Broadway play in New York the night before my surgery, and then back to the hotel to attempt sleep. I was scheduled to report to the NYU Surgical Center at 8:00 a.m. the next day.

I felt that I was in good hands. First, I trusted in the Almighty. After all, I was in His hands all my life, and today was no different. And G-d was going to guide the doctor's hands to do the best job for me. The day of the surgery, the nurse and anesthesiologist were surprised at my joking manner. I was simply so relaxed and confident that I was in good hands in every way possible. I knew that if I had to go home to the heavenly Father that day, it was all good. The only reservations I had about that possibility was in leaving my wife and sister, whom I love dearly. But, I was comfortable. The nurse said I was unbelievable. I said, "Be gentle."

Everything came out fine that day. The cancer was confined to a lower lobe, hadn't spread, and was removed. Now, in 2012, nearly nine years later, I'm still fine. All through the ordeal of diagnosis, treatment, and surgery, I never doubted that I was in G-d's hands.

* * *

102

Blessings

I've been blessed with good people all around me my whole life. The attitudes I have now reflect those that I've held all that time. I have always believed that no matter what the situation, we need to look at the bright side. I know it sounds trite, but I believe that G-d will see me through. The enjoyment I get from being with people, working with people, and helping people is tremendous. I feel that's why the Almighty has put us here on earth.

I enjoy my life, my work, my goals. I told my wife, Annie, that I could never retire. What I do every day is not work, it's a lifetime dream. Most people work at a job to earn money, and so many people worship money, too. They bring home a paycheck without enjoying what they do. But I love what I do and couldn't think of leading my life any other way than laboring for and with the wonderful people of the Jewish Renaissance Family of Organizations.

* * *

Afterword

The Jewish Renaissance Family of Organizations continues to grow and spread its reach within New Jersey and outward to the world. As more and more people receive our services, know of our plans, and meet the good men and women who carry out our missions, I am always asked to tell my story. In the course of a few months, I will usually relate parts of this narrative dozens of times. Writing down my memories, thoughts, and motivations to create this book seemed like the right path now.

And that path always directs me back to my family. I won't repeat their stories—you just have to turn back the pages to read them—but I will remind you of the spark that Grandpa Hymie mentioned to me so many years ago. The spark that has flared over and over in Perth Amboy, around Middlesex County, in our medical center on Hobart Street, in the Newark Public Schools, in Ukraine, Israel, Hungary, and Cuba, now shines for the beleaguered people of Haiti.

There will always be another chapter to write as long as there are people in need of assistance. We will always reach out. When the call for help resounded from the earthquake that devastated the island nation of Haiti in January 2010, the Jewish Renaissance Foundation and Jewish Renaissance Medical Center responded. We immediately sent a group of eight doctors and nurses with medical supplies. Our little team provided primary emergency and surgical care to the ravaged survivors in Port-au-Prince.

Since that January we have made other trips. Each time we brought medical personnel, medications, sorely needed eyeglasses, and hope to a people who, nearly ten months after the catastrophe (as I write this) are still without a source of potable water, permanent shelter, hospitals, schools, orphanages, or electricity. I have accompanied most of these medical missions and can attest firsthand that never was the need for Grandpa's spark more needed and more urgent.

The situation was crucial for the Haitian people. The first medical team we sent flew into very bleak conditions. That team of eight doctors and nurses experienced the same crude and dangerous living conditions as the people they were going to treat. They slept on the floor of the ramshackle remnants of a building they were using as a hospital. They performed surgeries right outside that ruined building. Patients lay on the pavement. And these doctors and nurses suffered the same hundred-plus-degree heat and scarcity of supplies as their patients. In fact, food and water for that first team ran low. One of the nurses had to make a run (in a makeshift truck-taxi called a "tap-tap") to the tarmac of the International Airport in Port-au-Prince to get food and water, because the hospital delivery had not arrived. These dedicated, selfless people spent a week operating under the most difficult conditions, providing a wide range of primary, pediatric, and obstetric medical care for approximately five hundred adults and two hundred fifty children. After that week, the first group of doctors and nurses left; the Haitian people could not.

I really had my eyes opened during my first trip in March of 2010, when I accompanied a team of eighteen doctors and nurses. Sleeping in a tent (in an over-crowded, noisy, makeshift tent-city), using primitive lavatory facilities, showering under a trickle of water, and attempting to stay hydrated in excessively humid heat way over a hundred degrees were daily feats of endurance and stamina. During this trip, those eighteen medical professionals saw and treated around two thousand patients in one week. The Haitians were already suffering from a huge range of health problems that were complicated by the catastrophic injuries sustained in the earthquake. Aside from post-traumatic emotional and physical difficulties, we saw people with heart problems, diabetics with no medications, those with numerous long-term untreated illnesses, and people with neglected vision problems. We brought a few thousand pairs of eyeglasses with us, and our optometrists were set to examine patients' vision. We attempted to match them with corrective lenses. We worked with the most dedicated Haitian doctors and nurses. We left after that trip feeling some sense of accomplishment. We have initiated bold projects and established the infrastructure to put in place some enduring and positive improvements for the Haitian people.

Dr. Goldsmith with the children and International Airport Police Commissioner, Justin Marks, in the old school, Tabarre, Haiti. Mr. Marks maintained the school for the children in the earthquake's aftermath, July 2010.

Dr. Goldsmith handing out uniforms to the school children at the school in Tabarre, July 2010.

These projects occupy a multi-faceted trajectory. In Léogâne, the Jewish Renaissance Foundation is committed to constructing a medical center, a children's safe haven, and school, on a parcel of land donated to the project by the municipal government. Nearby, we have acquired land with coastal access on which we'll build affordable housing for the citizens of that area. We also have plans to construct a factory, where the sections for those modular housing units will be made. Aside from the obvious benefit of creating low-cost housing, the factory will give us the opportunity to create jobs and offer vocational training on-site.

Dr. Goldsmith with his "little girl" in the old school building, 2010. Each of Dr. G's visits includes a smile-filled reunion.

* * *

It's with a great smile that I can now report (in 2012) that the Jewish Renaissance Foundation's first school is built, open, and serving over one hundred children in the town of Tabarre, right outside of Port-au-Prince. With a two hundred thousand dollar grant from the Merck Foundation, we helped construct a school building that took the place of a tiny haphazard structure made of tin panels scrounged from ruined buildings. That old ramshackle school structure offered little protection from the elements, had no bathrooms, no running water, and few supplies. A Haitian engineer oversaw the project and the local workers to complete the new building. The Jewish Renaissance Foundation has supplied the children and staff with uniforms, footwear, and ongoing medical treatment.

The brand-new school the Jewish Renaissance
Foundation helped build with a grant from Merck.

We have also collaborated with Foursquare Church to accomplish another monumental task. This passionate and devout group dug a well at the school in Tabarre. Now the site has toilets with running water, plus a water spigot where the school and town can draw clean water. Our collaboration with these wonderful people benefited all the children in many ways. Without a source of clean running water, these children were constantly at risk for dehydration, cholera, and other waterborne diseases. Foursquare Church helped us provide the school with a source of clean water, and we have helped them at their school and orphanage with their monumental task of providing medical aid for the children under their care.

One other area of collaboration is noteworthy. Ms. Deborah Burnell and her English 4 students at Mathis High School (Mathis, Texas) raised funds for school supplies, which they shipped to the Jewish Renaissance Foundation school in Tabarre. These high school seniors caused a huge ripple in the lives of the children still suffering the aftereffects of that devastating earthquake. We were so moved by this effort. Today's American teenagers are often portrayed and highlighted in the media as the "Me Generation." Sometimes it seems as if twenty-first-century teens are more interested in a pricey pair of sports shoes than anything else. Ms. Burnell's seniors have proved this false. They are making a big difference for children they don't even know.

We are going to try to help kids become more like Ms. Burnell's seniors. The Jewish Renaissance Foundation is currently developing the Youth Ambassador Corps so we can take students to Haiti to meet the children they are helping. We want them to see the results of their own hard work. It would be a gigantic experience for them to see the resilience of these small children in Haiti who respond with such excitement and gratitude for the items most American kids take for granted. The plan is underway for them to produce a documentary film about the children of Tabarre. We're hoping their efforts will show their peers back in the US how the Haitian children are coping like champions under such difficult circumstances.

Mission accomplished. The new school (with clean running water, uniforms, and school supplies) brings smiles to the children and Dr. Goldsmith, Tabarre, Haiti, 2012.

Dr. Goldsmith in the brand new school with his kids, Tabarre, Haiti, 2012.

I could continue to describe our Haitian projects. However, if you read the newspapers, the Jewish Renaissance Foundation's own newsletter, or go to our website (www.jrfnj.org) you will realize that I have only touched the surface of the Jewish Renaissance Foundation's involvement in that country's return to normalcy and health.

As you finish reading this book, know that the work of the Jewish Renaissance Family of Organizations, Grandpa Hymie's spark and nickel, and our worldwide reach continue to move from one heart to another. My wish is for you to take away a sense of compassion, kindness, love, and understanding of the needs of humanity. I hope you realize that you too can make a difference. Consider this book my nickel for you. What are you going to do with it?

Made in the USA
Charleston, SC
28 October 2012